300 QUESTIONS DREs ARE ASKING

About People and Programs

Gail Thomas McKenna

PAULIST PRESS
New York, N.Y.
Mahwah, N.J.

**Also by Gail Thomas McKenna
published by Paulist Press**

THROUGH THE YEAR WITH THE DRE

Copyright © 1990 by
Gail Thomas McKenna

Library of Congress Cataloging-in-Publication Data

McKenna, Gail Thomas, 1940–
    300 questions DREs are asking : about people and programs / Gail
Thomas McKenna.
      p. cm.
    ISBN 0-8091-3185-4
    1. Directors of religious education—Miscellanea. 2. Christian
education—Miscellanea. I. Title. II. Title: Three hundred questions DREs
are asking.
    BV1531.M28   1990
    268'.1—dc20
                                        90-36673
                                           CIP

Published by Paulist Press
997 Macarthur Boulevard
Mahwah, New Jersey 07430

Printed and bound in the
United States of America

CONTENTS

Introduction 1

About People

1. **Team Ministry.** Can Too Many Cooks Spoil
   the Broth? 5
2. **Pastors.** Friends or Foes? 17
3. **Catechists and Helpers.** Or, What Am I Going To
   Do With All These Volunteers? 31
4. **Religious Education Boards.** Are They With Us
   or Against Us? 47
5. **Support Groups.** We Can't Do It Alone. 59
6. **Personal Needs.** DREs Need Loving Too! 69

About Programs

7. **Administration.** Introducing the Computer into
   Religious Education. 81
8. **Children's Programs.** How To Make
   Them Easier. 93
9. **Youth Ministry.** Bring In the Teens! 105
10. **Adult Education.** We're Never Too Old To Learn. 119
11. **Family-Centered Programs.** The Family That Stays
    Together 131
12. **Sacramental Preparation.** Let's Get Parents into
    the Act. 143
13. **Summer Activities.** What About *My* Time Off? 159
14. **Liturgy.** Let's Make Those Special Liturgies
    Special. 171
15. **Publicity.** When You've Got It, Flaunt It! 183

Dedicated to the memory of
my dear father- and mother-in-law

PAUL AND ELEANOR McKENNA

who returned home to God.
Their prayers and sufferings
nourished me in my own faith journey
as this book was being written.

Introduction

I am a Director of Religious Education—a DRE. In fact, I've been a DRE for over twenty years—and I love it! During these years I've had the opportunity to minister to a wide range of parishes in the midwest and the southwest, and in several overseas military parishes. They have been exciting years as I've seen the church grow from the post-Vatican years to the present day.

In 1983 I began writing about my experiences in religious education for the popular religious education magazines. And in 1986 Paulist Press published my book, *Through the Year with the DRE: A Seasonal Guide for Christian Educators*. My intent was to give DREs—especially those just starting out—practical helps for managing their programs throughout a typical year. The book laid out a master plan which could be adapted by all DREs for their particular parish program.

As I conducted workshops around the country, I realized there were many questions that my book left unanswered—particularly questions concerning working relationships and program planning. This not only gave me a direction for a followup book, but also a practical format—using questions and answers.

I have divided this book into two general areas—people and programs. I further subdivided these sections into chapters, each containing twenty questions and answers, for a total of three hundred questions.

In part one I concentrate on the people who make up the world of the DRE—the pastor, the pastoral team, support groups, and volunteers. "How to fit into the pastoral team?" is a timely question in an age where the church is moving away from strong clerical leadership to shared authority by the clergy and laity. And there's also the often-voiced concern, "How to work in harmony with the pastor."

Every DRE looks for the secret to recruiting and keeping good volunteers. Chapter 3 explores this issue and answers sensitive questions such as "How to fire a volunteer" and "How to get teachers to attend meetings."

The final chapters in part one deal with providing support for the DRE through religious education boards and other DRE groups.

Part two begins with questions concerning the different programs the DRE is involved in. It opens with a look at administration, introducing a time-saving helper—the computer. And it moves into the different levels of programming—for children, teens, and adults, and the total family unit.

The R.C.I.A. (Rite of Christian Initiation of Adults) has heightened our awareness of the need for good sacramental preparation integrated with liturgy. Chapter 12 takes this into account as it looks at our programs for the sacraments, while Chapter 14 focuses on the importance of liturgy.

Finally, I felt it appropriate to consider an area DREs tend to minimize—publicity. If we believe we have a good product, a worthwhile program, why are we so reluctant to use every means to advertise?

Using a question-answer format, *300 Questions . . .* can be a handy reference for the DRE. The division into chapters according to personal relationships, age groups, and types of programs makes it easy to find that quick answer to your particular need.

The church is always changing, we are always changing, and our questions or our answers, for that matter, will not remain the same. But for now, these three hundred questions should answer the needs of the DRE who ministers to the church entering the decade of the 1990s. And if this book helps the DRE in this challenging work, it has fulfilled its purpose.

I am grateful to my husband, Jerry, who patiently edited each page and chapter of my work before its submission. I am also indebted to the many DREs who have enriched my ministry and helped me find answers to their questions. May we never stop searching, questioning, and growing in the journey of sharing our faith.

1
Team Ministry
Can Too Many Cooks
Spoil the Broth?

The 1980s opened the church to a new phenomenon—parish staffs working as teams. Words like "parish team" or "pastoral team" are becoming commonplace on bulletin covers and in parish programs. Quite a change from a church where "pastoral" was limited to those ordained to the priesthood. Today the church is hiring professional laity to help pastor the community. Who composes this team, and how does the DRE fit in? These and other questions will be addressed in this chapter.

1. What is a parish or pastoral team?

The parish or pastoral team is the group of adults who work with the pastor in the day-to-day ministering to the parish community. This team is usually composed of the pastor, his associate(s) and other hired professionals. Unlike the parishes of the pre-Vatican church, directed exclusively by ordained clergy, the pastoral team combines the gifts and talents of both clergy and laity.

2. Are all the professional workers on the parish staff part of this team?

The members composing this team vary from parish to parish. In some instances, this group is very small, including only the pastor, the associate, and the DRE, while in other situations this team will also include the deacons, the parish liturgist, ministry coordinator, youth minister and the school principal. The secretaries, administrators, bookkeepers, and janitorial workers usually come under the category of "staff" rather than team.

3. Isn't there a danger of causing division among parish personnel with team members and non-team members?

Yes, this is a very sensitive area and one that should be dealt with from the beginning. When a parish moves into team ministry an education process must take place. All hired personnel should be invited to a meeting. During this initial gathering the team concept should be explained using graphs and charts. The key issue is the importance of everyone working together for the good of the parish. Those who are in the position of making policy and running programs should compose the pastoral team. Other employees should see their function as necessary in supporting the work of the team. If you move into a parish where team ministry is already in process, become familiar with the operations of each member.

4. Where does the DRE fit into this team?

The DRE has a key role in this structure. Religious education is an integral part of parish life. With the collective resources of the other members, the DRE will be better able to assess parish needs and plan religious education programs to fit these needs. In a parish team set-up, you work *with* rather than under other key players.

5. If everyone on the parish staff is doing his or her job, why bother forming a team?

Two heads are better than one! For years our attitude has been, "You do your job, I'll do mine." But isn't it healthier if we all work together? If everyone is doing his or her job, all the better! Working as a team enables everyone to update on what's happening in the parish and brings support from the other members of the team. As we meet regularly, we'll get to know each other—hopefully keeping the lines of communication open. It's good to know we're not out there alone!

6. Should the deacon(s) be invited to be a part of the pastoral team?

Absolutely. Whether your deacons are paid or volunteer workers in your parish, they must be included on the pastoral team. They have been assigned to your parish to assist the pastor and in some cases substitute in his absence. They should not be kept from this team, which in many ways is an extension of their pastoral role.

7. How often should the team meet to be effective?

Once a week. If this is not possible, then at least twice a month. This is true no matter what size your team or parish is. These meetings should be scheduled for at least ninety minutes. You'll find in the beginning that you'll need to allow more time. Gradually your meetings will follow a format and develop a practical timeframe for the group.

8. Should the team and staff also schedule regular meetings?

Yes. But these can be on a monthly or bimonthly schedule. Because these groups work together, they too must have an opportunity for keeping the lines of communication open. After the weekly team meetings, it's important to keep the other staff members informed on matters that will affect them. It's also good to bring the entire team and staff together for socials and celebrations throughout the year.

9. Should there be times when the team gathers for a longer, more intense meeting?

Yes. You need this time for building community and trust among the members of the group. If you can, schedule a full day or

---

SAMPLE SCHEDULE FOR TEAM MEETING

2:00   Team gathers.
          Opening Reflection on the scriptures for the follow-
          ing Sunday.

2:15   Sharing: Part 1: *What's Happening*
          Each team member shares past week's programs,
          areas of interest to parish, and any concerns.

          Part 2: *What's Coming*
          A look at the calendar week to follow. Input from
          team members on their programs.

3:15   The administrative staff joins the team for com-
          munication of week's programs. Members of staff
          are invited to ask questions or share any problems.

3:50   Closing Prayer.

---

weekend away from your parish meeting place. You may even
want to have a professional facilitator work with the group in this
initial stage. This day will set the groundwork for the meetings that
will follow each week throughout the year.

10. What issues should the team be addressing?

Look at the pastoral needs of the parish. The team should focus
on how to meet these needs through liturgy, education, and service. In focusing on these issues, the team can use its energy for the
total good of the parish. Hopefully this will keep them from getting bogged down in too much "nitty gritty."

SCHEDULE FOR SPECIAL ANNUAL TEAM MEETING

Friday Evening:

Gather at parish and carpool to retreat center or other meeting area away from the parish.

7:00   Unpack and get settled. Depending on the weather the group can take a walk, watch a video, or sing and talk.

10:00   Evening Prayer Service.

Saturday Morning:

8:30   Gather for breakfast.

9:00   Morning prayer.

9:15   1st Session: Our faith journey—talk and activity.

10:30   Coffee break and sharing session (one on one).

11:30   Group sharing.

12:00   Lunchtime and relaxation.

1:00   2nd Session: Our Parish Vision—talk and activity.

2:00   Group sharing of vision.

3:00   Setting goals for the team and for the parish.

4:00   Evaluations.

4:30   Closing prayer service.

5:00   Relaxation—happy hour.

6:00   Supper.

7:00   Departure center and return to parish.

(If the group meets only one day, follow the Saturday schedule.)

11. Who sets the agenda and controls each team meeting?

Many teams rotate leadership of team meetings among themselves. The leader is usually responsible for setting the agenda. However, this is not the only way to decide the weekly agenda. Some teams prioritize needs to be addressed at these meetings, taking some items each week. Or each member can create his or her own agenda—items and issues he or she wants to cover. The important thing to focus on is parish issues, not personal concerns, when setting your weekly agenda.

12. I've heard about "reflection time" being scheduled into the weekly meetings. What does this mean?

Team meetings are more than business meetings. And although we are accustomed to begin our parish meetings with a prayer, these gatherings can use even more preparation. If we open with a period of reflection—using scripture, music, readings, and quiet— we become more aware of the meaning of our ministry. We realize we need the Lord in his work. I've noticed how often we rush into the work at hand, as if we just can't afford to set aside ten or fifteen minutes for prayerful preparation.

13. How do we tell our parishioners about the work of pastoral teams and their value to the community?

First, parishioners should know who is on this team. This can be done by placing their names on the weekly bulletin cover. And when possible, place their pictures on the parish bulletin board. When a parish is forming a team, it should inform the people about this new type of parish leadership. And from time to time, it's a good idea to use the media—bulletins, parish newspapers, announcements—to highlight the role of the pastoral team.

14. How can we bring the parish school (where one exists) into the pastoral team?

Invite the principal to be part of the parish team. This not only gives the school a voice in pastoral concerns, but it gives the school a communication link with this group. In so many parishes there is a separation of school concerns and religious education programs. Providing a structure where principal and DRE come together regularly helps unite these programs.

15. How does the pastoral council function within the framework of a pastoral team?

The pastoral council and the pastoral team should be very compatible. Unlike a parish council, concerned mainly with business, the pastoral council is a visionary group. It is created to function as an extension of the pastoral team because it seeks to define the needs of the parish community. The pastoral council should support this team by informing them of the parish needs.

16. What are some of the problems that arise when you begin to form a pastoral team?

Try something new in any parish and you're opening the door to problems, real or imagined. But it can work! First, you need the willingness and cooperation of everyone on this team—beginning with the pastor—in order to make it work. Unfortunately, many clergy resist this concept of shared ministry. They are products of a hierarchical church, and want to cling to this approach for their own reasons. And even when all the members do accept this notion, many resist the large investment of time it demands. But to work effectively, we need to allow for mistakes, for trial and error, for growing pains.

17. Will my role as DRE change when the parish follows the parish team approach?

No. Your role and job description should be basically the same whether you are working in a parish with or without a pastoral team. However, the way you carry out your ministry may be affected. In a team, you're not alone. You will have a vested interest in the team and some of your energies will be directed toward its success. But it will reap its rewards! You can turn to your team members for support and help in creating good religious education programs for the parish.

18. What are some of the advantages of parish team ministry for me as a DRE?

We have already addressed some of these—support from others, input into the religious education program, a feeling of community. For over fifteen years I did not have this network. And then I moved into a parish with a pastoral team. I have seen how it has added a new dimension to my personal life as well as to my professionalism. We can become very myopic in our vision of parish needs if we work alone, putting our interest only into programs *we* initiate. Working closely with others in a team approach forced me to look at total parish needs, widening my vision and sensitivity to the parish. At the same time, it has given me a sense of accountability—to the team and the parish community. In fact the entire church community reaps the benefit of a good parish team as it "models" church.

19. Are there any disadvantages?

There can be, if the team can't work well together and yet they are forced into a team situation. When this happens, you'll find yourself expending more psychic energy on the group than on its mission. As a result your particular ministry can suffer. If there is a lack of trust or support within the group, the team concept can cause more harm than good.

20. Is it important to know what type of parish team ministry exists in the parish before I apply to work there?

If you don't want to commit yourself to team ministry, you certainly do not want to apply for a job where this is the form of parish leadership. Not all parishes are convinced of the value of teams, and many pastors prefer to continue as they have for so many years. However, don't close the door to this option just because you've never experienced it. I was in religious education many years before I became part of a team. I'd never want to return to the "old way."

2
Pastors
Friends or Foes?

One of the key ingredients for a successful and satisfying ministry as a DRE is a good working relationship with the pastor, while one of the most frustrating experiences for a DRE is not being understood or supported by the pastor. Attend any conference or workshop of DREs and the question eventually emerges, "But what do you do if the pastor doesn't buy into the program?" Although we tend to blame the pastor for problems in the parish, this is not always the case. I've worked with many wonderful pastors over the years. They not only have been supportive of my ministry but also have become lifelong friends. As you will see, the key is keeping them informed and involved in your programs. In this chapter we will look at how to build a positive working relationship between the DRE and the pastor.

1. As a DRE am I accountable to the pastor or some other parish organization?

As a DRE you work for the parish and are answerable to the pastor. In some parishes the religious education board or the pastoral council has some influence in selecting and hiring the DRE. And because of this the members feel they are responsible for assuring that the contract is being fulfilled by the DRE. These councils are established to advise the pastor. They are not meant to be power organizations. Unfortunately, I've seen situations where they assume this power to the dismay of the pastor—and the DRE.

2. Why should I meet the pastor before I sign my contract?

Each parish is unique, and many DREs move into a parish knowing only its boundaries and some general characteristics. It's important that you and the pastor meet each other because you will be working together in the parish. If you have the opportunity to talk before a contract is signed, many questions and problems can be resolved. You can determine the pastor's expectations. And the pastor can inform you about the personality of his parish. Sitting down with the pastor and talking is much better than reading all the materials on the profile of the parish. One of the major problems of DREs and pastors is a lack of communication. If the partnership can be founded on the premise of open communication with each other, you're off to a good start!

3. Won't there be a problem when I request a salary higher than the pastor's?

There shouldn't be. If your salary were lower than the pastor's, there would be a problem. Remember, in most parishes the pastor is provided his home, the upkeep of his car, and other benefits. These are not included as salary, which is paid over and above these needs. Because of this the pastor's salary is not very impressive. Our intent here is not to argue whether the pastor receives a just wage, but rather if the DRE is getting a just wage. You will usually find that all full-time parish employees are receiving a higher salary than the pastor. It's not recommended that the decision on what the DRE receives is dependent on what the secretary or administrator gets. When this situation arises, it only creates problems. Most dioceses have guidelines for the salary of a DRE. These guidelines should be researched to decide the salary for the new DRE.

4. How can the pastor know my areas of responsibility?

Your areas of responsibility as a DRE should be clearly defined in your job description accompanying your contract. However, pastors rarely see these job descriptions. That's why it's essential for you to discuss these areas of responsibility together. Some pastors want to be involved in all the sacramental preparation classes,

---

**WAYS TO INVOLVE THE PASTOR
IN SACRAMENTAL PREPARATION PROGRAMS**

Invite him to:
1. Welcome the parents and candidates at the beginning of the sacramental preparation program.
2. Lead the community of parents and candidates in the rites in preparation for the reception of the sacrament, such as the rite of enrollment of candidates, blessings, etc.
3. Present the theology of the sacrament for the parents.
4. Visit the classrooms of the children or teens who are preparing for the sacrament.
5. Be present for the rehearsal or final preparations before the celebration of the sacrament.

---

while others prefer to have their director conduct these classes, making only an occasional appearance. The same is true in regard to classes for children, teenagers, and adults. With deacons now helping out in parishes, they too must be brought into the equation and understand how they fit into the different areas.

5. My pastor tells me: "I won't interfere with your work as long as you're doing your job." What does he mean by this?

The message given with this statement can be interpreted in a variety of ways. One message could be, "I really don't have time to be concerned with your area; that's why I hired you." Not a very positive approach for the DRE, who, like all normal adults, needs affirmation. Or these words can imply, "You're so competent as Director of Religious Education, I give you full reign in that area of our parish." Flattering—but does that mean you're in this *alone?* And yet another way to interpret this statement is: "I'll only get involved with your work if you mess up!" None of these statements are very reassuring to the DRE. When the pastor says anything along this line, the DRE should respond, "I think we need to talk!"

6. It seems that some DREs are a threat to their pastors. Why?

It could be because they are usually women! Unfortunately some pastors have a difficult time accepting the reality of the Vatican II church and women's role. But another reason, and probably a more common one, is the fact that the DRE, male or female, can be more educated and more in tune with the church of today. There is an emphasis on priests' renewal and updating, but some pastors failed to respond to these programs. Most DREs coming into the parish have just completed either an undergraduate or a master's degree program. They begin talking a different language because of their education, and pastors can become very leery of their theology and methods if they haven't updated themselves.

7. How can I keep the lines of communication open to the pastor?

Form pastoral teams and have weekly meetings. Since both the pastor and the DRE are key players on the pastoral team, it's a good time to keep both parties informed on what's happening. If a pastoral team is not practical it may be necessary for the DRE to schedule time during the week to meet with the pastor to keep him informed. The DRE has to develop a workable arrangement for keeping the pastor informed. Some pastors prefer a more flexible approach, that is, having the DRE stop in the office whenever the need arises to discuss matters on the programs. I feel it is the DRE who needs to take the initiative when it comes to sharing all the religious education programs. The one message you *don't* want to hear from your pastor is, "I never know what's happening in religious education."

8. If I were to concentrate on one area, what is the most important thing I can do for my pastor?

I've found that DREs are in a unique position working with the pastor. Together we share a common ministry—bringing the "good news" to the parish community. If we stand behind and support our pastor we can be a source of strength for him in his ministry. It's lonely at the top, and no one knows this more than the pastor. If we're working at his side, at least there's someone he can turn to in those difficult times when no one really understands. The reason I have become friends with so many of the pastors I've worked with is because we've worked through those rough times as well as the good times in forming community in the parish.

9. How can I assist the pastor in the sacramental programs in the parish?

This is one area most DREs are prepared to work in—the scheduling, organizing, and directing of sacramental programs. For years this was handled by the priests or the ordained ministers in the church. Now DREs have become the experts in providing good parent programs combined with children's classes in preparation for the different sacraments. This is especially true in regards to preparation for reconciliation, first eucharist, and confirmation. But the pastor should not be excluded from these programs of preparation. He should be invited to participate by either giving a presentation to the parents or working with the children's groups. This helps the children get to know their pastor—the person they'll be approaching as they receive these sacraments.

10. What should I do in situations where parishioners refuse to follow the religious education guidelines and approach the pastor directly for exceptions to the policy on sacramental preparation classes?

This is a *delicate* situation. Anyone who has been a DRE can tell stories of times when parishioners turned to the pastor because they didn't like the guidelines or rules they were asked to follow. In some instances those asking for an exception had a legitimate reason. However, there are too many cases that don't fall in that category. We need to remember that with any guidelines there are exceptions, and to be sensitive to families who are returning to the church and can't understand all the new rules. Most of all, it is important for the pastor and DRE to have an understanding on how these "exceptions to policy" requests will be handled.

11. What message are we giving to the parish community when we can't work well with our pastors?

There are going to be instances when the DRE and the pastor just can't work well together. But this doesn't have to be known beyond the pastoral team. If this situation becomes known to the parish community, it can lead to "taking sides." There will be those who side with the pastor, and those who support the DRE. This isn't healthy in a community which ideally works toward unity. You don't have to agree with everything your pastor says or does, but you owe each other loyalty and support.

12. How can working with pastors change our understanding of them?

It's a whole different picture when you move into the inner circle of parish life. When you work closely with a pastor, you begin to see that he is human with limitations just like other human beings. Even more than that, you realize that he has human needs too—the need for affirmation, love, and friendship. And you are in a situation to be a *friend* as well as a co-worker. In fact, I've known DREs who have stayed in the same parish for years because of the friendships that have developed with the pastors they are working with. Over the years I have met many wonderful pastors whom I cherish as friends today.

13. Does the pastor want me to work in the parish school?

That depends. Some pastors want the DRE to coordinate the total religious education program for children. That means working in the schools as well as setting up programs for children in the public school. However, there are parishes where the school program system is completely independent and the pastor prefers that it continue in that mode. For years pastors and principals have worked together for the education of children. DREs are relatively new to this field. Unfortunately, they aren't always a welcome newcomer.

14. I find our pastor torn between his loyalty to the parish school and support of the religious education program. Where do I fit in as a DRE?

This is a problem. Many DREs have experienced being in the middle of a similar situation. The parish school has been around from the beginning. The religious education program is a recent addition to parish life. It shouldn't be an either/or situation when it comes to the pastor's support. Each program is contributing to the educational needs of the parish. Because the larger part of parish funds goes toward the maintenance of the school, we sometimes conclude that's more important. It's necessary that the pastor, DRE, and school principal work *together*. If they can meet on a regular basis and discuss their programs and problems, the pastor is more likely to be supportive of both programs. Then it's not a case of the DRE and principal competing for the pastor's allegiance.

15. How can DREs and pastors of different parishes work together?

Unless you are working in a rural parish isolated from other parishes, there will be parishes nearby. It's a good idea for the DRE and pastor to come together periodically and share their experiences. If you are in a diocese where parishes are divided into deaneries, you'll be able to use the deanery meetings as that time to share. In the past, deanery meetings were limited to the priests. Now they are opening their doors to others on the pastoral teams—DREs, administrators, liturgists, and coordinators. These joint meetings can be scheduled quarterly, while the regular priests' meetings are monthly. We can learn from each other as well as share parish programs and materials. We can work together in setting guidelines for sacramental preparation programs.

16. Are there other areas in which the pastor and DRE can be a support for each other?

If the DRE and pastor can support and encourage each other to attend programs that will benefit them, there can be a healthy balance between active ministry and personal enrichment. We all need continual renewal since the changes of the Vatican II church are affecting parish life. Even though many DREs have recently completed studies in theology in preparation for their ministry, others begin with practical experience but limited theological studies. As for the priests, the gamut is also wide—from those who put their energies into the daily parish duties with no desire to attend education programs to those who sign up for *every* program offered for renewal. Pastors and DREs should encourage one another to participate in programs that will enrich their personal lives and improve the parish ministry.

17. Why should the pastor welcome the DRE on his staff?

I would hope the answer to this question would be evident. The DRE should certainly be a person who can ease the burden of the pastor's duties. No longer do parishes have the luxury of many assistant pastors on their staff. There are even parishes who must share pastors. The DRE has been educated to take care of areas that were previously handled by one of the assistant pastors, such as sacramental preparation classes, providing religious instruction for all those seeking entrance into the church, and organizing programs to meet the needs of everyone in the parish. A DRE who can concentrate on these areas is definitely a welcome addition to any parish.

18. I have made a sincere effort to work with my pastor and it just hasn't worked out. What should I do?

You must be true to yourself. Many times a DRE will begin working in a parish only to find in time that there are problems in working with the pastor. You can't just walk out the door because everything is not going well. After all, a contract is a contract. If possible, you and the pastor should sit down and talk. But if this is not feasible, you should make *every effort* to continue to work in the parish until the contract is no longer binding. There may be situations where this isn't possible. Then, in this case, you should look at the terms of the contract concerning notice for termination and seek professional help in pursuing this route.

19. Should I renew my contract if my pastor is being transferred? I'm not sure I can work with his replacement.

There are many factors you should consider when it comes to renewing your contract each year. The ability to work well with the pastor does make your job easier. But it's not the only ingredient for success as a DRE. When pastors are reassigned, there is an element of uncertainty as a new pastor moves in. Most pastors would welcome a DRE who was familiar with the parish needs. Until you work with the new pastor, you are in no position to judge whether you can work well together. If you find there is a personality conflict or other factors which make your job unbearable, you don't have to renew your contract after the year has ended. But until you've given it your *best,* I'd advise you to continue in the parish with the new pastor, being a source of support and help in the transition.

20. What are the good things that are happening in our church because of DREs and pastors working together?

A pastor and a DRE both have many gifts to bring to the community they serve. When they join together to serve the parish, these gifts increase. Because many DREs are women, they can bring that added feminine dimension to the ministry. In the church of today, with the shortage of ordained ministers, we need to call upon the talents of the laity. Men and women who have become educated to work in the religious education programs of the parish have much to offer the community. There is the good they do together in sacramental preparation and adult education programs. There are also many ways, in the daily routine of parish life, that this team is effective—counseling parents, affirming volunteer workers, and providing programs to foster good Christian living, to name a few. There will always be parishes where DREs and pastors find it difficult to work together. Let's hope they remain in the minority.

3
Catechists and Helpers
Or, What Am I Going To Do With All These Volunteers?

At the heart of any good religious education program are the men and women who have come forth to share their talents. It is the volunteers who give of their time and talent week after week, year after year, who are the treasure of every program. As DREs we must never lose sight of this fact—our volunteers are our greatest resource! How to bring them into our programs, meet their needs, and show our appreciation of them is the focus of this chapter.

1. Every parish has its "faithful few"—the group of men and women who are involved in every activity and can always be depended upon. Is this true in the religious education program as well?

You'll find that the religious education program is no different from any other parish activity when it comes to depending on that "faithful few" for help. As I talk to coordinators around the country, I realize how important it is for them to have one group who are the mainstay of their program. There is enough turnover in teachers and helpers as it is. And there are many times when you can turn to this group for support and feedback on the program. After all these are the people who are in the middle of the action, and many of them have been in the parish longer than you have. However, the effective DRE should never be satisfied with this limited number but should *continually* recruit new workers.

2. The ranks of my religious education staff are dwindling. How can I reach out and bring in new workers into my program?

There is nothing more effective in bringing new volunteers into your ministry than the *personal* approach. All the finest art on posters, or clever ads in bulletins, won't begin to draw in new workers as effectively as a personal invitation from *you*. I feel that one of our biggest challenges in working with volunteers is making them feel we really want and need them. Just as Christ called his followers by name, we too should invite each person by name.

3. Are there "prime times" for recruiting new teachers and helpers?

Yes, there are the times each year that naturally lend themselves to recruiting more teachers and helpers. First there is *springtime* when we assess our needs for the coming year and find out if any of our teachers will not be returning. This is also a good time to evaluate the area your teachers and helpers are already working in. Some may want to move into new areas. Many times those who have been aides or helpers are ready to become teachers themselves.

If you are having a *summer program,* you have another opportunity to look for new workers and invite them into your year-round program. In this short period of a week or two many will volunteer to help because of their children. I've often had some of these adults and teens approach me after the summer session asking to become part of the regular program.

You can also recruit at the time families *register* to become part of the parish community. As you explain the religious education program you can invite them to become involved in it. It's amazing how many will take you up on this invitation, especially if you are enthusiastic about your program.

Another key time for adding more workers to your program is the annual *commitment Sunday.* At this time most parishes not only ask for a pledge amount for stewardship, but also for a commitment of time and talent to the parish. One of the categories for commitment is in the area of religious education. It is so important that you follow up on contacting those who have said "yes" to working in your program. I've often heard this complaint from parishioners, "I checked that I'd be willing to work in the program but no one called me. I guess they have enough workers." We *never* can have too many volunteers in our business. Don't expect folks to keep saying "yes" if we ignore their response the first time.

4. It seems that every year prior to starting up classes there is an urgent request for teachers needed. How can I avoid this last-minute appeal?

How often in late August or early September do we hear either the pastor or the DRE making a desperate plea, such as "We need a teacher for Grade 5, and our high school program still needs two couples for this year's group," hoping that someone in the pews will step forward. How does a parish react to these panicky pleas? Inevitably someone responds. Sometimes it's the woman who was going to take a year off to enrich herself, or the man who has never taught but knows he can quickly fill in rather than close the class down. The list is endless on how each parishioner will react to the plea. But someone *always* comes forth because we never hear: "Due to lack of response we are not having fifth grade religion classes." I contend that this last-minute appeal can be avoided if the DRE looks at the program as always being reinforced with new volunteers, with a surplus to draw from. Yes, there will be those August appeals once in a while due to the unforeseen transfers and circumstances which necessitate someone pulling out who had planned on remaining. But these are the *exception* and not the rule. There will be recruiting for each new year—that's inevitable. Our concern should be to avoid last-minute requests where we may be just looking for a "warm body" in order to carry on. Remember, we need time to train and work with our volunteers *before* they walk into the classroom. The message: Recruit continually!

5. Although our main concern is usually for good catechists, what other workers are needed for a successful program?

The workers behind the scenes are essential men and women who take care of the many nitty-gritty tasks necessary for the smooth running of any program. Their value cannot be underestimated. Too many DREs have the mentality that *they* should double as "runners" for their teachers—available every minute that classes are being taught to take care of any needs. After all, the teachers are busy in the classrooms. They can't be troubled with other details. But did you become trained and educated as a DRE only to become a distributor of supplies? Your role is to be *visible* to your catechists while they are teaching—present to support them and encourage them in their work. You need to be available for them, to be able to drop in on classes, to show your interest in their work and to have some contact with the children in the program. And in order to do this you need lots of adults and teens who will assist you in the administrative tasks. Someone needs to take up attendance slips, deliver needed supplies, pass out materials teachers have requested, and even lock up at the end of the day. I've also found it helpful to have a person or two in charge of the AV materials. When the teachers want a particular film, filmstrip, or video, this person can be in charge and free the teacher from the concern of setting up and showing the materials. In some programs there are snacks for the little ones. Again your volunteers who want to help, but don't feel comfortable teaching, can be called into service. It's really a challenge to you as a DRE to assign all who are interested in working in your program into the right area. A good DRE welcomes all helpers into the program aware of the gifts each person has to offer to the community.

6. Are there certain qualities that we should look for in accepting a volunteer to teach?

When someone comes forward to teach, we need to discern his or her gifts and readiness for the task. This can be done through a personal interview, a written questionnaire, or a combination of the two. (Note the sample questionnaire in this chapter.) We should look for men and women who are models for our young people. A faith-filled person who loves children will be more effective than a professional person intent only on teaching doctrine. Through our initial contact, we'll become acquainted with our volunteers—learning their talents and the areas where they would like to work. At the same time we have the opportunity to see if they have the qualities necessary to be catechists—an openness to learn and grow, an understanding of the church today, the ability to work with others, common sense, and, of course, a love of their faith. We need to be alert to those men and women who want to join our team of catechists in order to do "their own thing" because they don't agree with the curriculum. We cannot sit in judgment, but we do have the responsibility of guiding and directing our volunteers to the work they are best qualified to do. As DREs we should pray to the Spirit for help in this process of discernment.

7. Once we have found willing volunteers, what types of in-service can we offer our workers to prepare them for their ministry?

One of our main concerns after recruiting our teachers is training them. Although many of those who volunteer are not new to the teaching ministry, each parish has its own approach and style. You want your teachers to be comfortable as they enter their classrooms. Plan to gather your teachers and helpers at least one month before classes begin. This gives them time to prepare for

CATECHIST INFORMATION SHEET

Name: _____ Spouse's Name: _____

Address: _____ Zip: _____

Home Phone: _____ Work Phone: _____

☐ ☐ ☐

Children: (Names & Grades) _____ ____, _____ ____,

_____ ____, _____ ____, _____ ___.

Birthday Date: _____ Anniversary Date: _____

Hobbies: _____

☐ ☐ ☐

Religious Education Information: On Class Preference

Area You *Prefer* To Work In: _____

Reason(s) You Choose This Area: _____

_____

Time You'd Like Your Class To Meet: _____

Person You Would Prefer To Work With: _____

Inservice and Background

Former Teaching Experience (in R.E.): _____

_____

Former R.E. Training (Inservice in parish, workshops, conferences, etc.):

_____

_____

For our planning purposes and scheduling:
Time Most Convenient for You To Attend Workshops and Meetings:

Evenings: _____ Best Night: M T W TH F Saturday Morn: _____

How can the R.E. staff be of service to you in your ministry?

_____

_____

their first class and it gives you time to make any changes in teacher assignments or scheduling. At your initial meeting you might want to set goals for the year. Schedule a follow-up meeting about a week before classes begin to go over class routine, schedules, supply requests, and other teachers' needs. This is also a good time to pass out class lists with phone numbers. I encourage my catechists to contact their students before the first class—it's a personal touch that means a lot. By the time you open doors for the first class, everyone should be ready—if you've done your job well during this initial in-service period.

8. I feel it's important to make your teachers and helpers a community. Are there some keys to making this happen?

I've walked into parishes where catechists have been teaching for years but they never knew the person who taught in the next room. Each Sunday they'd religiously teach their lesson, then depart. What type of community experience is that? We need to concern ourselves not only with informing our teachers, but also with forming them—into a community. This can be done through experiences of praying, working, and playing together. I like to begin the new year by gathering the teachers and helpers together for a social. This can be a cookout, a potluck, or an ice cream party. Throughout the year I try to plan other occasions to come together for fun and sharing. I remember a teacher who signed up every year, and she confessed that she did it so she would be included in the parties.

9. Am I the only person responsible for in-service for the teachers and helpers in the program?

Yes. However that doesn't mean you can't turn to others for help in providing in-service. In most dioceses there are catechist-formation programs. These programs usually call upon the "expert" catechists and DREs to present materials which will help teachers in theology updating as well as practicum. As a DRE you'll want to encourage your teachers to take advantage of these programs. Another source to turn to is your own teacher community. Some of your teachers are blessed with talents and gifts in leadership and in special areas. Use them. In larger programs you can ask your teachers to be responsible for a specific area at a meeting, easing your load. We are sometimes hesitant to call upon our teachers to help, yet many of them have the wisdom of years in the classroom.

10. How can I get my teachers to meetings and workshops throughout the year?

I often hear the complaint from DREs: "I spend hours preparing for a teachers' meeting and only a few show up." It is discouraging and a very real problem we face when we are working with volunteers. They are giving of their time as they prepare and teach their lessons. Can we ask more? I think we not only *can* ask more, but *must.* The two key factors are scheduling and making the meetings worthwhile. Before you schedule a meeting, consult your teachers about the *best times* for them. And don't forget to look at the local school calendar. I've found that a telephone call reminder shows your teachers that this meeting is "still on" and important. For our part we must be honest and evaluate our meetings. Are they worth giving up an evening at home? If they are, our teachers will make the effort to attend regularly.

11. How does one "fire" a volunteer?

In a very *gentle and loving way.* Anyone who has been in the DRE ministry for over a year has no doubt encountered this dilemma—

what to do with volunteers who just aren't working out. They haven't signed a contract so there's really no hiring or firing. And yet as director you must take some action before more harm is done. It could be the case where discipline in the classroom is out of control (too much or too little), or adults working with teens and trying to teach their own pre-Vatican theology, or any number of situations where positive faith-sharing is not happening. We need to be sensitive to both parties—the students and the teacher. And when it's a situation of the teacher being the problem, we need to talk to the person. Not everyone has the qualities needed to be a good catechist. However, anyone who has volunteered to help should not be turned away completely when it's not working out. A good DRE will take the time to guide this person into another ministry where he or she will feel comfortable and needed.

12. What is the most important thing I can do for my volunteers?

Support and encourage them in their ministry. There is nothing like affirmation for bringing out the best qualities in a person. I've watched teachers and workers grow from insecure but willing workers to confident and productive ones. It's so important to show your care and concern for each person who is working with you. Remembering birthdays and other special family days is a sign that this person is important. I try to greet the teachers as they arrive for their classes. It's in these brief encounters that I can learn of any problems or personal needs in the family. At these times we show our teachers and helpers that we truly care about them.

13. Why do some people come back *year after year* to help in our programs?

I feel it's their commitment and their belief that God has given them the gifts and talents for this ministry. It certainly can't be the paycheck they receive. As I travel around the country giving work-shops to catechists I like to ask them how many years they have been catechists. It's thrilling to see the number of veterans—twenty years plus—in every audience. In sharing their personal faith with others, they say that their own faith is deepened. And the joy they experience as they work with God's children renews their faith in the goodness of the world. No wonder they keep coming back!

14. Should I consider paying my catechists for their service?

In some parishes it's a policy to give the teachers a small stipend for their services. This is to offset the cost of babysitters or give them a little extra to take the family out to breakfast on a free Sunday. However, most parishes don't follow this policy because of budget limitations or their belief that the teachers really don't want money for their services. There are many other ways to say "thank you" that can mean more to your volunteers, such as giving gifts at Christmas or at the end of the year, or having appreciation dinners at least annually.

15. I've met DREs who always have enough teachers. What's their secret?

It would be nice to say because they're such good DREs. Maybe that's part of the reason, but there are *many* reasons why some DREs have enough teachers. Some factors that influence this are the type of parish you're working in, the classroom facilities, how many years you've been in the parish, the priority of religious education, and the way you recruit and work with the teachers. I've already pointed out the need to be continually recruiting for potential workers. I think a more important issue is how we work with the teachers in our programs. A caring, supportive DRE, sensitive to the needs of the volunteers, usually retains them. There will be circumstances that cause teachers to leave. But if your turnover is exceptionally high, it might be a good idea to evaluate your relationship with your teachers.

16. Can I "burn out" my teachers?

Yes, you certainly can, especially if they're good in other areas besides teaching. For some reason we are good at over-tasking the same two percent of the people in the church. And this is true no matter what size the community is—two hundred or two thousand families! We won't burn out our teachers, however, if we just allow them to teach and not take on numerous other projects. That doesn't mean they can't step out of their role as teacher and assume a new position in the program. I like to invite some of my more experienced catechists to coordinate certain areas of the program, moving from the classroom to administrative work. There are also times that I'll ask teachers to help coordinate a specific project, such as an Advent day or a special liturgy, besides their teaching. As long as this is kept to reasonable requests, your "burnout rate" will diminish.

17. Are there advantages to using the team-teaching approach?

I am convinced that this is the best approach when working with volunteers *at any level.* For teaching, you have your built-in substitutes—people who can take over the class. And they already know the children. With teens you are providing more role models to meet their various needs. And it's even a good disciplinary tool—while one person is teaching, the other is free to take care of minor disturbances. I encourage my experienced teachers to take a new volunteer as an aide or assistant. It's invaluable for on-the-job training, and many friendships have developed between team members as they worked together as catechists. Finally, there's that feeling of support in the classroom while you are teaching—you're not in this alone. I've always thought the fact Jesus sent his disciples out *two by two* says something to us.

18. Should I schedule retreats for my teachers too?

Definitely. Just as we ask our teachers to continually share their faith by giving to others, we must give them an opportunity to be refilled and nourished. Unfortunately I have found that many teachers don't take advantage of this opportunity. When in-service is scheduled for the year, they're ready to sign up for all the practical sessions to help them. However, they will pass up the opportunity to grow through a retreat experience. It's good to schedule at least one retreat a year. I've had retreats in late August, mid-year in January, and at the end of the program in May. There are pros and cons for each time period. It's during these times, when we can combine prayer, work, and play, that community happens.

19. How can my teachers help me evaluate my program?

Many times our teachers are in a better position than we are to see the good that is going on in the religious education program. They can also see the weak areas that need attention. We need to look at our regular programs at least once a year. Our special programs—summer programs, sacramental programs, etc.—should be evaluated at their conclusion. (Note the sample format in this chapter.) It's smart to take time either at the meeting or after the program for filling out the evaluations. This will increase your chances of getting the completed forms. But be ready to accept negative as well as positive comments if you're serious about improving your program.

END-OF-THE-YEAR PROGRAM EVALUATION

What did you like about our program this year?

_____

_____

_____

What would you like changed next year, to make it even better?

_____

_____

Materials: YES NO
1. Do you like the teacher materials you are using? ☐ ☐
2. Do both teachers need the lesson plans?   ☐ ☐
3. Do you think the student materials are adequate? ☐ ☐
4. Do you use the take-home sheets each week?   ☐ ☐
5. Did you have the necessary supplies for your lessons? ☐ ☐

Meetings:
6. Were the monthly teacher meetings helpful?   ☐ ☐
7. Would another time be more convenient? (If yes,   ☐ ☐

   mark alternate time: _____)
8. Would you attend inservice meetings from the dioce- ☐ ☐

   san office? (If yes, what day is best: _____)

Future Plans:
9. Do you know anyone not presently teaching who   ☐ ☐
   would be interested in joining us next year? If yes,

   Name: _____ Phone: _____
10. Will you be returning next year for another year of ☐ ☐
    sharing your faith with the children or teens?

          GOD BLESS YOU! YOU'RE ALL WONDERFUL!

20. In what ways can I show my teachers and helpers how much they are appreciated?

There will be the *special* times when we gather to show appreciation. This is usually the end-of-the-year appreciation banquet or evening. Sometimes this is part of a *total* appreciation dinner for all parish workers. If your budget allows, it's a good time to give a small memento or certificate to your teachers as a thank you for their year's work. If you can't give something to everyone, single out those who are either retiring or moving out of the program. Another time of the year we can show our appreciation is during the season of Christmas, combining a celebration with small gift-giving. In some parishes where this isn't possible, at least send your teachers a card and enclose some type of gift. It's certainly not the gift as much as the thought that they are being remembered and are appreciated. Be sensitive to any opportunity throughout the year to say "thanks" for being part of the religious education program.

4
Religious Education Boards
Are They With Us or Against Us?

Religious education boards are becoming an integral and functional part of religious education programs. They are composed of men and women who are interested in the religious education program and want to make a difference. In the early years these boards were concerned with setting standards and assuming responsibility for the religious education programs. Today, however, there is an interest in forming boards to act as visionaries—drawing up mission statements and long term goals. This new style of organization can be a valuable resource for the DRE and all who are involved with the religious education programs.

1. What is the purpose of the religious education board?

The religious education board is a vehicle for providing a vision for the total religious education program. Through its efforts, long range planning can take place. And the people of the parish are given a voice in creating policies and goals for the religious education program. It can be a support body for the DRE and the religious education staff.

2. I seem to be getting along fine without a religious education board. Why should I want to create one?

In your ministry you'll need all the help and support possible. It's difficult to stand alone. This is one of the main reasons for having a religious education board. The decisions coming from this group will be respected because it speaks as a body and not one individual. The group usually has a position on the pastoral council, and as such is a voice for you as a DRE. This is one group who can make your job easier—make time for it on your monthly calendar.

3. In our parish I've noticed that some members use their membership as power positions. Can this be kept under control?

Unfortunately politics and power plays can even creep into church programs. As we select members for the board, we must make every effort to choose those adults who have the genuine interest of the program at heart. Your first members should be appointed by the pastor and members of the parish staff, while the subsequent members will be elected by the parish at large. It's a good idea to schedule religious education board elections at the same time as the annual pastoral council elections.

4. How can I know the role of the religious education board as I move into a new parish?

If you begin working in a new parish where a religious education board is already active, your first move is to meet with the chairman of the board and become knowledgeable about its operation. Because not all parishes follow the same guidelines in setting up boards, you may experience anything from a tightly knit group of "concerned parents" to a very charismatic and visionary group of parishioners. And depending upon the pastor and the pastoral team, this group can be very influential or just existing nominally. Whenever you're changing parishes, it takes time to begin to know your parish and your support groups. You may not like the structure of the board and want to make changes. But before you get ambitious, why not accept the situation and work with the existing group? You'll want to put your energies into listening and learning. If this group has been in existence for some time, there must be a value. In fact, this just may be the group that made the decision to hire you.

5. Does every parish have to establish a religious education board?

In our Vatican II church, there are very few "have to" statements. Although more parishes are establishing boards, there are many where they are non-existent. I've known pastors who feel that these boards just get in the way and refuse to allow them to exist. And I've worked in parishes where these boards were very important for the well-being of the religious education program. If there is a parochial school with its own school board, the religious education program is more apt to have a counterpart in its religious education board.

6. I'd like to establish a religious education board in our parish. How do I begin?

First of all, this is usually not the decision of the DRE alone. It should be a joint decision of the pastor and the religious education staff. As a DRE you certainly are in a prime position to initiate a board if your parish is lacking one. Once this decision is made, the first step is to begin recruiting members. These should be parishioners who have knowledge and interest in the parish religious education program. After a sufficient number selected have given their consent to be on the board, it's time to schedule a meeting and provide a direction.

7. How can this meeting set the right direction for our new board?

This initial meeting is the key to giving the religious education board its purpose and direction. And because it is important, you might want to find a qualified person who can give the proper perspective through a presentation on designing a mission statement and creating goals. There are experts available to help groups develop skills in interpersonal relationships as well as skills in setting goals and policies for programs. If we don't take advantage of these professionals, our group may find itself drifting with little sense of direction, or getting involved in areas beyond its jurisdiction.

8. How many members should be on the religious education board?

It's better to start small—about six members—and build. After the first year, you might want to ask two or three more to join the group. As a DRE you're automatically part of the board. And if you have other coordinators, such as for youth, adult education, etc., they should also be included. The maximum number for your board to work effectively should be twelve.

9. How long should members serve on the religious education board?

Each board can decide on terms; however one or two years is a reasonable time. After the initial board is appointed, you'll be electing future members. For continuity on the board, it's best to stagger the elections, with one-third of the board rotating each year. If you follow this pattern, no one will be on the board permanently.

10. Is there a way I can make sure that our religious education board covers all areas of religious education?

For years, much of our energies in religious education was concentrated on the youth. We can no longer limit our vision to only the youngest in our midst. And it's the religious education board that should support these efforts to reach out to the entire parish community. One way of assuring that each level of education is considered is to divide the members of the board into the three interest groups: children, teens, and adults. While all members work for the total vision of religious education, each group takes on the added task of looking at the needs of their level.

11. How can we keep the parish informed on what the religious education board is all about?

One of the major problems of parish organizations is their inability to communicate to the parish at large. It seems that if you're not involved, you're not informed. Most parishioners know what organizations are included in their parish because of reference to them in the Sunday bulletin. Don't they deserve more? A good time to highlight the education board is at election time, when you are asking everyone to vote for representatives for this board. This can be followed up by short articles about the activities of the religious education board in the parish newspaper or other media within the parish. It's a good idea to have someone on the board responsible for public relations.

12. I keep hearing the term "mission statement." How does a group write such a statement?

A mission statement is a statement of identity—it tells who you are, what you believe, what you value, and your overall goals. However, it's only recently in the church that we have begun using this terminology. In fact every *parish* should have a mission statement. It's from such a statement that your policies, goals, and objectives are drawn. If your group is unfamiliar with the process of drawing up a mission statement, it would be advisable to seek

---

SAMPLE RELIGIOUS EDUCATION PHILOSOPHY

1. We believe that religious education is a lifelong process.
2. We believe that the faith development of adults is our primary concern.
3. We believe that parents are the primary educators of their children.
4. We believe that is is our responsiblility to support the parents in this role.
5. We believe that our educational programs should be developed around scripture and liturgy.
6. We believe that both adults and children should be aware of the meaning of their Catholic roots.

---

expert help. Once you have drawn up a mission statement make sure it gets wide distribution throughout the parish.

13. Is the philosophy of a religious education board different from the mission statement?

Yes. The mission statement is one complete statement giving a vision, while the philosophy will be spelled out in several statements. Actually, the philosophy sets the environment for the mission statement to become a reality. The philosophy can be expressed in about six statements which are the springboards for setting goals for your program.

14. Why are long term goals important in any religious education program?

There's an assurance that programs will have continuity when you establish long term goals. Without them, your program is limited to the term of the DRE. And with the steady turnover of DREs, our parish programs can suffer. Setting five year goals for the entire program allows the religious education board to act as a visionary. Once goals are set, it's up to the DRE and other coordinators to implement these goals in programs they create.

15. Is there any relationship between the goals of the religious education board and those of the parish?

Yes. Remember that the religious education board doesn't function as an entity unto itself. However, it's through this board that the teaching ministry of the parish is implemented. When the religious education board is creating goals, it needs to look to the larger goals of the parish for direction. Hopefully, the pastoral council has led the way by outlining these goals. Once goals are formulated, they should be distributed to members of both groups. And periodically reports should be given on the progress being made toward attaining each goal.

16. Is the religious education board represented on the council?

Yes, the chairman is usually the representative on the council. However, this will vary according to whether you have a parish council or a pastoral council. In a parish council structure all of the parish committees are usually represented. Your religious education board chairman will represent the education committee. As a

DRE you would probably be an ex-officio member. In a pastoral council structure your religious education board will be represented in the area of ministry, representing the teaching ministry. And you as a DRE would be included with the administrative staff. No matter what approach your parish takes, you and your religious education board have a position.

17. Is it true that my job as DRE gets its directives from the religious education board?

If the religious education board is functioning as we have already described, setting up a philosophy and goals, you should have a clear sense of your responsibility. Once goals are set, programs must be created to achieve these goals. That's your task! Unfortunately this has not been true of boards in the past. In fact, they were known to move into the DRE's territory—setting up programs, testing their effectiveness, and in some cases evaluating the DRE's job performance. Is it any wonder that such boards were not welcomed by the DRE?

18. How can we conduct meetings effectively?

If you've been involved in any committee or church organization, you no doubt have experienced those meetings that went on and on. They might have had an agenda, but even that got lost. It's so important to remember the value of time and not abuse it by lengthy meetings. If you're in charge of the meeting, there are certain points you'll want to keep in mind for conducting a successful meeting. Although I'll only highlight some of the skills, you might want to refer to books written exclusively on this subject.

POINTS FOR CONDUCTING A SUCCESSFUL MEETING

1. Get there early to set up the room, check AV, erase blackboards, etc.
2. Arrange chairs to suit the meeting, i.e. in a circle, seminar style—around a table, or in rows.
3. Begin and end your meeting on time, limiting it to one hour . . . an hour and a half at the most.
4. Supply all members with an agenda, note pads, and pencils.
5. Keep control—don't let others go off in tangents from the agenda.
6. Allow ALL members to be heard without one or two monopolizing the meeting.
7. Have coffee, tea, or light refreshments available for the group.
8. Allow time for fellowship, either at a break time within the meeting or immediately ater the meeting.
9. Provide babysitting if possible when needed.
10. Be clear about dates and responsibilities between meetings.

---

19. How can we include prayer in our monthly meetings?

We're all familiar with beginning a meeting using one of the traditional prayers of our church—usually led by the pastor—and then hurriedly getting down to "business as usual." But this hardly places us in a prayerful mood. Today I'm seeing this approach change as groups are taking time for reflective prayer and meditation—about ten or fifteen minutes—before rushing into business. With the help of meditative music and readings, or using verses from scripture, we can place ourselves in the presence of God. This period of quiet time—time where we place our needs and anxieties before God—can do much to place us in the right spirit for the work ahead.

20. Why should I as a DRE be so concerned about all these aspects of religious education boards?

As a DRE you are in a position to cause change. I have talked to many DREs who have good religious education boards as well as those who simply endure their religious education boards. Any knowledge that can help us improve our situation is knowledge worth having. If you've never researched the area of religious education boards, you're depriving your ministry of a support network it needs. No longer can we be expected as DREs and pastors to carry the weight of the total education program *alone*. Having a board of dedicated parishioners to affirm you, support you, and give you direction in your ministry is something worthwhile and invaluable.

5
Support Groups
We Can't Do It Alone

Almost every parish has one person in the position of director of religious education. There may be others who work under the DRE such as a youth minister, an elementary coordinator, or a religious education administrator. But ultimately it's the DRE who is responsible for the overall religious education program in the parish. Those who share in this ministry need to turn to each other for support and encouragement. Today DREs are coming together for this reason. Let us look at how these gatherings can be organized and how they can help us become better DREs.

1. Are there any support groups for the DRE within the parish network?

Most DREs I know try to turn to their pastor for the support needed in the ministry. But this should only be the beginning of the support network. The parish or pastoral team should be there, as well as the pastoral council, to back the DRE and religious education program. Each DRE should have a following, i.e. a group of parishioners who believe in the work of the DRE and are always present for help and support. As a DRE you need others—and they need you. Seek these people out. Even Christ didn't go into his ministry alone.

2. Can I turn to other parish organizations for support in my work in the religious education program?

Yes, you'll want to approach all the leaders of the other organizations when you begin working in a parish. One of the chief causes of lack of support from others is usually due to a failure in communication. The pastoral council, the liturgy committee coordinators, the women's altar group, and the men's club are only some of the organizations your parish may have. And all of these groups are already in existence to serve the needs of the parish.

However, you don't want to contact these groups only for the help they can give. You will need each other as you work together for the good of the parish.

3. How often should I meet with these parish groups?

Certainly more than once. That's usually where we make our mistake. We tend to think it's enough to make contact with an organization, explain our program and make known our desire to work together. It's a good start, but we should do more. I know we can't go to every committee meeting every month. But if we plan ahead, we can arrange our schedules to attend the different organization meetings throughout the year.

4. Can DREs form their own group for support in their ministry?

Yes. There are already many DRE support groups meeting throughout the country. They come together for support, encouragement, and mutual growth. If you're in a large city, your group will probably be organized to include different subdivisions of the city or deaneries of the diocese. If you're in a rural area or a small city, your group will cover a larger area and the DREs will have to travel farther to get together.

5. My calendar is already overcrowded. Is this type of meeting worthwhile?

A DRE's calendar is always overcrowded. It's up to you to set priorities for your monthly activities. If you limit your commitments to serving others and never build in some time for your own needs, you'll find your ministry undernourished and overex-

---

FIVE REASONS FOR DRE MEETINGS

1. **To Support** . . . one another. We aren't in this alone. And it's good to meet with others who are traveling the same road and sharing the same ministry.
2. **To Renew** . . . ourselves. We should leave these gatherings feeling good about our ministry, happy to be part of this group!
3. **To Form a Network** . . . working together and helping each other. We have talents and resources to share.
4. **To Enrich** . . . our personal and professional lives by bringing in other professionals into this group for ongoing education.
5. **To Relax** . . . and have fun! If we form community, we'll want to have times of celebration together.

---

tended. A meeting with others for support *is* necessary if you follow this principle of making time for yourself. This support and encouragement you get from other DREs will enable you to continue during difficult times.

6. How often should our group of DREs get together?

This depends on how far your group has to travel for a meeting. If you're in the same city, it's advisable to meet at least once a month. If you're separated by larger distances or live in a rural community, your meetings can be scheduled on alternate months or quarterly throughout the year. This is something that can be decided upon at your initial meeting.

7. Should these meetings be scheduled for a full day?

Most DREs would be hesitant to set aside a full day each month for this type of meeting. For groups gathering each month, a couple of hours should be sufficient time to conduct your business, allowing time for some socializing. However groups who meet quarterly will need a full day to take care of their business. Within that day, the lunch and coffee breaks will provide an opportunity for the DREs to become better acquainted.

8. What are the advantages of scheduling meetings over lunch?

The greatest advantage of this scheduling is that it doesn't take too much time from your day at the office, and it provides a pleasant atmosphere for eating lunch with fellow DREs. I once met with a group of DREs who voted on lunchtime for their meeting time. We would all gather about 11:30 a.m., eat lunch, visit, and begin our business around 12:30 p.m. We were usually returning to our parishes before 2:00 p.m. Using this time frame, we were able to be at our offices most of the morning and part of the afternoon. Because we were meeting over the lunch hour, it didn't seem to infringe on our busy day.

9. Since all the participants are DREs, who leads this group?

This will differ according to the group. If someone from the central diocesan office has been appointed as leader for your group, that decision is made. In most situations, however, your group will be self-directed. And then it's the group who will decide the leadership. Some groups like to rotate this role, giving each DRE the opportunity to host the meeting, set up the agenda, and lead the meeting. Others prefer to elect a chairman for the year who acts as leader for each meeting and works with the group in deciding the agenda. Under this plan the other DREs alternate hosting the meeting at their parishes.

10. What should be included on the agenda?

This is a good opportunity to inform DREs on diocesan policies, events and programs. Your contact from this office would address these issues. It's also a good time to share your individual programs. This area can be a very sensitive one. I've been at meetings when this sharing turned into a "can you top this" event. The purpose of sharing is to *learn* from each other. It takes a good leader to direct this aspect of the meeting, making it a positive experience for everyone. These meetings can also provide further education for the group. Some groups have worked together to set guidelines for sacramental programs. It's up to each group to set its own agenda.

11. Do these groups have the authority to set guidelines?

If we remember that setting guidelines is not the same as making rules, there's no problem. When DREs come together to write up directives for their area, they are usually doing this to provide some unity in their programs. Guidelines and directives are needed in the area of sacramental preparation. If all the parishes are making similar requirements, we can discourage "shopping around." Anyone working in sacramental programs knows that this is a common problem.

12. What about bringing other resources to this group?

A good idea! If we spend all our energies at these group meetings evaluating our programs, we can limit our vision. Inviting someone to the group to give a presentation or work with the group can help the members stretch to new dimensions. There are usually a group of professional men and women in every diocese you can refer to for qualified speakers.

13. I've heard some DREs invite their pastors to their gatherings. Is this a good idea?

Anytime we can bring pastors and DREs together, we open one more avenue for communication. We widen the vision of religious education beyond our parish to include the larger church of many parishes. This helps the DRE and pastor not only to see how they work together in their parish, but also how their program affects the other parishes. I've often heard pastors speak of feeling left out of the religious education process. By bringing DREs and pastors together for these meetings, each benefits from the expertise of the others.

14. I don't think my pastor would come to a DRE meeting. Do you have any suggestions that may help get him there?

If you believe your pastor should be there, it's up to you to get him there. I've found that by personally inviting my pastor to join me at these meetings, he's more apt to respond. If this is the first meeting of this type, he may beg off—not realizing its importance. But for too many years DREs have been encouraged to "do their thing" and not bother the pastor. We can no longer take that stance. So much of the work we do in our parish depends on a good working relationship with our pastor.

15. Should the agenda be different when pastors are invited to the meeting?

This will depend on whether pastors are coming to your meetings regularly or if this is a one-time affair. If the pastors only come to one meeting, you'll want to make the most of this opportunity.

Take time for the DREs and pastors to become acquainted with each other. It would be good to have a printed agenda ready to hand to the members as they arrive. A brief summary of the purpose of this group, along with comments on what you are presently working on, will help put your guests at ease. If you would like interaction between the pastors and DREs, this must be programmed into the meeting. If the pastors do come often, you would no doubt follow your usual agenda, inviting their input.

16. Could I bring other coordinators to these DRE meetings?

Your other coordinators—elementary, youth, and adult—should always be welcome at DRE meetings. And although they may not want to attend every meeting, there will be some meetings that appeal to them. For instance, when discussing sacramental preparation programs, the coordinator who is working with those programs should be invited to participate. This is a good preparation for coordinators who are planning to move into the role of DRE.

17. How can I get a DRE support group in my area?

If your area does not have a support group, you may want to get one started. Contact your diocesan office with your proposal. They should be able to help by supplying the names and addresses of the DREs in your area. Decide upon a date in the next four to six weeks and invite the DREs to an initial gathering. Since you are taking the first step, you'll want to host the first gathering. Your first meeting should be one where you get to know each other and decide whether you'd like to unite and form a support group. Basic decisions such as how often you'll meet, where you'll gather, and the purpose for your group should be taken care of. Once you've agreed to continue meeting, you're off to a good start.

18. What is the connection between these area DRE meetings and the diocesan office?

The diocesan office is organized to be of service to the religious education personnel in the diocese. Most offices have found they need the help of those in the field to do their jobs well. One of the ways they can do this is by organizing groups of DREs into local areas where they can be a support group to each other. Some dioceses set up these groups and assign a member of their staff to facilitate them. Others do not get directly involved in the organization of these groups although they support this endeavor.

19. Even though there are small gatherings for DREs, I would like to see situations where the larger group of DREs of an area come together. Is this a possibility?

Yes. And this is happening on both the city and the diocesan level. This is one of the services your central diocesan office should provide for you. If it's not happening in your area, it might be time to call your main office. All the smaller support groups should be invited to participate in days of retreat, renewal, and enrichment. It's within this larger community that DREs can experience a sense of unity in their ministry.

20. What is the greatest value of DREs meeting together?

I have found that the greatest value is the wisdom shared that helps both the novice and the veteran DRE. The new DRE will learn more from those who have walked this journey than from any book or course on the subject. For those who have spent years in this ministry, there's a sense of pride in sharing their accomplishments. This is one audience who will listen to what works and what doesn't work.

6
Personal Needs
DREs Need Loving Too!

So far we have considered all the different people the DRE works with. Now it's time to look at the needs of the DRE. It's so easy to get caught up in ministering to others that we forget to take care of our personal needs. And then we wonder why we begin to feel physically and emotionally exhausted or, as the current catch phrase puts it, "burned out." Somehow we begin believing we're indispensable and without *our presence* the program just can't go on. We must be honest with ourselves and accept the reality that the church survived for years before we became DREs. I'm convinced that we will not only *survive* but will even *love* our ministry if we remember to take care of our needs as we respond to the needs of the community. What are some of the personal needs of the DRE and how can they be met?

1. My schedule is unbelievably hectic. How can I possibly find time to pray and reflect and still meet my commitments?

We make time for what we believe is important. If we truly believe prayer is essential to our ministry, we can't afford to leave it to chance. For example, I've always tried to include daily Mass in my schedule. When this hasn't been possible, I take a few moments at the beginning of a work day for quiet and reflection. Every DRE should decide what time and place is the best for quiet and prayer. It can be in the office or chapel at the beginning of the day, a quiet walk at lunchtime, during a jog at the end of the work day, or some other break time. If we can't take time for prayer, I think it's time to reexamine our priorities—and our profession.

2. Why is spirituality important for my ministry?

We are in a unique position. We are called to touch other lives almost every day. Others turn to us for spiritual direction, for guidance in matters of faith, and for help in their daily struggles.

Because we work in a leadership position in the church, they rightly expect to get some answers and help. We can be a means of grace, bringing others closer to God. But we must be people of faith, nourished by the Lord in order to give nourishment to others.

3. Can I take a "day off" during the week?

If you are on duty over the weekend, or are spending evenings as well as days in the office, you need a day off during the week. Our jobs don't fall into the Monday to Friday, 9 to 5 time frame. You'll find you're working more than a forty hour week—with no time and a half for overtime—if you don't build in a day off. There will be those busier times of the year when it's necessary to put in extra hours, but they should be the exception. There's something nice about taking a day off in the midst of the week, a day to do

---

TEN WAYS TO SPEND YOUR DAY OFF

1. Sleep in (when possible).
2. Go to Mass and out to breakfast (alone or with a friend).
3. Set a luncheon date with a friend.
4. Take a leisurely afternoon shopping trip.
5. Relax, put up your feet and read a good book.
6. Treat yourself to a movie, either alone or with others.
7. Visit an art gallery or museum.
8. Do something creative: write, paint, draw, do crafts or sew.
9. Take a leisurely drive, either alone or with a friend.
10. Go out for a quiet dinner or to the theater with your spouse or a friend.

those other tasks demanding our attention—shopping, house cleaning, and running errands. Sometimes I use my day off to have lunch with friends or do something relaxing. I've found that Thursday is the best day for me, but you need to look at your schedule to choose what day is best for you. I've met many DREs who are hesitant to take time off. They're concerned about all the work to be done and their need to be available. I can honestly respond that one reason I have enjoyed my ministry is because I've learned to take that necessary day off!

4. How can I guard against too many evening meetings during the week?

In a busy parish there are always many religious education programs, classes, and meetings scheduled in the evening. And even though you're involved with these programs and classes, you don't necessarily have to be present at *all* of them. As you schedule your programs for the month, keep in mind your availability. I plan to be at one meeting or class each week. During busier seasons I'll double my evenings out. But that's where I draw the line. We can delegate others to coordinate evening classes or represent us at parish meetings. We owe it to ourselves, our families, or our religious communities to limit our evenings at the parish.

5. I've heard others speak of a "Messiah complex." What does that have to do with my ministry?

When DREs begin to believe that they are indispensable and have come to answer all the needs of the parish, feeling like a savior to all, we have the beginning of the infamous "Messiah complex." It can so innocently creep into our ministry that we don't realize it's happening. The danger is we forget *whose* work we are about and begin taking undue credit. Or we become workaholics because there's so much to do and only we can do it! Don't get overconcerned about your limited time. Jesus had only three years to minister—and look what he did!

6. You make it sound so easy, but I have a hard time saying "no." Why is this necessary?

If you don't say "no" periodically, you'll soon find yourself at your wit's end. Just because you're working for the church doesn't mean you're *super-human.* If you're good at what you do, you may be asked to work in areas beyond your ministry. Be careful about overextending. Before you realize it, you could be on every committee in the parish and in the diocese.

7. What are some opportunities I can take advantage of to grow professionally during the year?

There are usually workshops, classes and lectures offered by colleges, the diocesan offices, and professional teams throughout the course of the year. They are scheduled on Saturdays, weekends, or evenings for our convenience. Most parishes will subsidize these opportunities for professional growth, since the knowledge from these can make your good programs even better. It's also a good idea to bring other coordinators and members of your team to these enrichment programs.

8. The question of attending conferences or conventions is a "sore spot" in my parish. Why?

They cost money—and the question arises, "Are they really worth it?" Conventions are routinely accepted in the business world, but they're looked on with suspicion among church leaders. And those who head the fund council or financial committee are the first to question their value when they study the request for funds. This is unfortunate, for I've attended many *outstanding* conventions at which I've experienced renewal and confirmation. It's also a great place to meet others who share in the struggles, the challenges, and the joys of being a DRE. However, it's important to share the wisdom from these conferences with others when we return to our parish. We need to let them see it was worth the time and money invested.

9. How can I decide which conference or convention to budget for each year?

You'll need to do a little homework, since you can't attend them all. There are usually national conventions scheduled regionally throughout the country. Although it's practical to attend the one in your region, it might not be the one that meets your needs every year. If it's a matter of cost, the main difference may be in air fare, and by booking early even that may be kept minimal. Getting together for room-sharing not only keeps the cost down but adds a special dimension of community to your experience. Since you're only attending one conference, it's important to search for and invest in the right one. You and your fund council will be surprised how cheaply this can be done.

10. How can I keep up professionally throughout the year?

One of the best ways to keep informed on what's current in religious education is by subscribing to the periodicals and journals in this field, such as *Catechist, Religion Teacher's Journal, PACE,* etc. Most religious education magazines address the needs of catechists and DREs. It's also a good idea to keep up with the current books published in your area. As leaders in our church, we need to be informed on all the changes in the church.

11. I never seem to get my work done during the day. Do you advise taking work home in the evening?

When I was a teacher it was normal to take work home. There were papers to grade, lessons to plan, etc. So naturally when I became a DRE I found myself taking work home—organizing class lists, checking through religious education materials, and other various tasks. However, it soon became evident that evenings in religious education were needed for meetings and classes and weren't free for work at home. I now find it better to leave office work at the office. You need time for yourself, and, unlike the teaching profession, a DRE's working hours can extend into evening without adding paperwork to it.

12. Do you advocate a summer vacation? If so, how long?

We all need time away from the job—time to renew ourselves, time to relax and move away from the duties of our profession. If you are putting all your energies into your job throughout the year and never take time to have fun, you'll soon find yourself exhausted and even disliking your job. How much time is allotted for vacation differs from parish to parish. It's not as clearly defined as a teacher's vacation of three months or a secretary's vacation of three weeks. It seems to fall somewhere in between these two categories. I've found that a month is the right amount of time to request for vacation in the summer. And the time to take it is when we aren't running programs or everything is slow. I advise new DREs to negotiate their vacation at the time they are hired and have it included in their contract.

13. Why are some DREs reluctant to take time off from their ministry during the summer?

I've never met a pastor who didn't take his vacation each summer. But I have met many DREs who feel they can't take a vacation because they are needed at the parish. Some stay because the pastor is gone and the parishioners need someone around who understands the parish. Others don't take time off because there are *always* tasks to be completed. Whatever the reason, I have a hard time accepting it as an answer to why they don't take time off. Our work during the year can become very intense, and as I have mentioned so often, we need to get away at some stage. If we don't, we will suffer the consequences along with our programs and the people we work with.

14. How can I use summertime for spiritual renewal?

The slower pace of summer lends itself to more time for renewal. It's a good idea to schedule a retreat for ourselves during this time. A few days devoted to our spiritual life is certainly not too much to ask. In our working with others we are usually leading and organizing retreats. Now we can attend one where someone else has done all the planning. Another way we can renew ourselves is by doing some spiritual reading. Again, this is often a luxury we aren't able to fit into our daily routine. Planning some quiet times to read and reflect can nourish us for our ministry.

15. I've heard of having a spiritual director to turn to for personal guidance. Is this something I should consider?

We used to associate spiritual directors only with religious life. Today, however, we see this area expanding to include the laity, and especially the laity involved in church ministry. If we are serious about our spirituality, we should use all the resources available to nourish it. This is one such resource—a person we can turn to for help on our journey of faith. Even though you may never have had a spiritual director, this may be the right time to consider choosing one. It can help you personally and in turn be a help in your ministry.

16. Where does one go to find a spiritual director?

Because this is still relatively new, there is not a vast amount of material on locating spiritual directors. You can approach your diocesan offices for information. However, many adults turn directly to a priest or religious with whom they feel comfortable for spiritual direction. There are also deacons ready to answer this need. Again, you're not limited to the ordained. There are many lay people working in the church who are willing to be a spiritual director. The important thing is that you're not only comfortable sharing with this person, but also willing to be open to the spiritual guidance and direction he or she gives.

17. How can I maintain a healthy balance between taking care of my personal needs and serving the community?

As DREs we are constantly being called upon to serve the needs of the community. That's why we entered this ministry. But I've found that taking care of personal needs is too often neglected. I think of the commandment "to love your neighbor as yourself" and feel that this applies to us as DREs. We must love the people we minister to—trying to meet their needs—as we love ourselves—meeting our needs. If we neglect the latter, the former is going to suffer. The needs of the community are always before us. But we must make a conscious effort to take care of our personal needs.

18. Should I actually schedule "me" time?

If you don't, you may find that you never end up with time for yourself. Each month, as you schedule your meetings and events, mark off a day or two for your own enjoyment or enrichment. This can be a social event, a trip, or even a visit with a friend. And respect that commitment as you do your others.

19. Are there other ministries I can become involved in to enrich myself?

Yes. Each parish has many areas of ministry beyond the religious education program. It's good to extend ourselves in those areas that appeal to us. I have always liked being a eucharistic minister. You may prefer singing in the choir or joining the prayer group or some other committee that interests you. This also shows others that we have a vested interest in the total life of the parish.

20. Why is it worthwhile to offer our talents beyond our parish commitments?

There is something very rewarding about ministering in new territories. I'm sure there's something to the "prophet in his own country" syndrome. I have been giving talks in parishes for many years. And I've always been affirmed in doing this. You don't have to be an expert to share with others. In fact, I was only in my second year as a DRE when I was first asked to give a workshop at a neighboring parish. We have so much to offer each other. And it's true that in giving, we receive.

7
Administration
Introducing the Computer into Religious Education

Administration of a religious education program can be time-consuming. Just keeping registration forms, attendance records, and sacramental data current takes time. And the larger the enrollment, the more paperwork there is. In some parishes you will have the luxury of your own religious education secretary and administrator. You may also have the use of a computer—a welcome time-saver. This will lessen your burden considerably, especially if you're expected to absorb the administrative tasks. How to stay on top of all—no matter what your situation—and also be available to those who need you is the subject of this chapter.

1. Each year we ask every family to fill out a registration card for religious education classes. Isn't there an easier way to conduct registration?

Yes. Create a permanent registration card that is good for at least five years. Then all you have to do is *update* it each spring before classes are over. This can be done by sending a letter to each family enrolled in the program. They return the lower part stating who will be returning in the fall and enclosing a partial or full registration fee. With this information the family cards can be updated in the office.

2. What's the best time to schedule registration if we're planning to begin classes in September?

For years I was caught in the August registration madness. With just two or three weeks prior to opening classes, there was hardly time to get the class lists compiled from registration forms. And then one year I decided to try pre-registration—that is, registration before classes had ended in May. What a difference! By June we were putting together tentative class lists. In August there would be registration *only* for new families in the parish, and these names could quickly be added to the proper lists.

3. I've heard that some parishes are putting all their registration on computers, but I don't know how to operate one. How long would it take to be trained to operate one?

There are many quick training courses available for the novice computer operator. Some are conducted at the local high schools through evening classes; others are scheduled at business schools or in the nearby colleges. I suffered from computer fear, having no knowledge of this new device. And so I decided to sign up for a four-week course in basic computer knowledge as well as one in word processing. It worked! After completing both courses, I was ready to try my skills on the computer at work. I transferred my typing skills to the computer, and the more I worked with it, the more comfortable I became. In fact, I used my PC to write this book. Using a computer *can* lessen your work load.

4. What are some of the advantages of using a computer over using a typewriter for my administrative tasks?

I have found that using a computer eliminates a large amount of paperwork. Since information can be stored on a disc, it is easy to recall. I can also save form letters needed in the program. These can be retrieved for repeated use. And they can be easily altered with a quick change on the keyboard. If I need multiple copies, I can readily print them out, easing the load on the copy machine.

5. My teachers complain that it takes a long time to take attendance each week. Are there any "tricks" to make it less time-consuming?

One method that works well with speeding up attendance taking is placing the names of your students on small cards. These are

---

RE: TASKS FOR THE COMPUTER

1. Compile class lists.
2. Complete registration information for students.
3. Record family entries.
4. Create letters to be sent home.
5. Keep student records up to date.
6. Retrieve names of children for specific purposes:
   a. To find children who have not received a sacrament.
   b. To make lists of children the same age, grade, etc.
7. Keep class attendance lists.
8. Make labels with family names, addresses for mailout.
9. Glean information about any special needs.
10. Record registration fees as well as other payments.

---

placed on a table by the entrance to the room. As the children arrive, they pick up their card and place it in the designated box. All the teacher or aide does at the beginning of class is pick up any remaining cards and mark those students absent.

6. If I follow up on absenteeism will it improve class attendance?

Yes, your attendance will improve and you may begin to understand why some students are absent. Many times it's a situation beyond their control. But the fact that you take the time to call gives the message that you care. If you have a large program to oversee, you may want your individual teachers to take care of following through on their students. However, it's important that they share their findings with you. No program is so large that you cannot be aware of family problems and situations affecting class attendance.

7. What can I do about tardiness? So much class time is wasted when children come in late.

There is no easy answer to handling tardiness. Many factors enter into getting children on time for classes. But like so many areas, parents will usually respond to what is asked. And if we stress the importance of coming on time and insist that classes begin on time, we're apt to get better results. At one parish we had our religious education classes in conjunction with the Sunday liturgies. Since class time was limited to only forty-five minutes, it was important that no time be wasted. After the first few weeks we noticed more and more children just wandering in ten and fifteen minutes late. Classes were being continually disrupted. We decided to initiate a "tardy" program. The children who arrived after the opening prayer were not allowed to enter the classroom. They were sent to "tardy tables" set up in a nearby hall for their lesson. Even though they weren't missing the lesson, they missed being with their classmates. In the weeks that followed, tardiness decreased to the point that the "tardy table" could be abolished— at least temporarily.

8. How can I avoid the last minute rush to get class lists to the teachers?

If you use the pre-registration system in the spring, you'll have a head start on class lists. When August arrives and you begin meeting the teachers, you'll be able to hand them at least a tentative class list. You'll only have to add the names of new registrations before the first class.

9. How can I generate lists of those eligible for participation when I begin preparation for first eucharist classes?

Since you know you'll need this information, you'll want to build it into your registration card at the beginning of the year. If you don't have the luxury of a computer, you can either color code the cards or leave them blank in the area marked for eucharist. This will help identify the children who have not received this sacrament. Pull these cards and send letters to the families inviting them to participate in your eucharist preparation program. This is an important letter, so you'll want to mail it rather than have the child hand-carry it. If you do have a computer, you can key in the proper code, which will in turn generate a list of those boys and girls who are the proper age to begin preparation for this sacrament and have not received it. If your computer is set up with the capacity of printing address labels, you're in business.

10. How can the computer help in providing sacramental data?

When you set up your registration cards you can program them with the different sacraments and have them coded to mark the sacraments each child has received. If you need more specific information, such as the date and place sacraments were received, you can place that information on their registration card and enter that in the computer as well. Much of the time we spent in the past on marking cards and class lists can be eliminated through the use of computer programming.

11. As a DRE am I expected to take care of all the administrative tasks in the program?

It depends. If you have the luxury of a secretary or administrator, count yourself blessed. When I began work as a DRE in the early

1970s, I remember the diocesan director telling us that every program, no matter how big or small, must have a secretary. If we didn't have a secretary, we would end up spending most of our time doing administrative tasks. And that's not what DREs are hired to do. Eighteen years later I hired my first secretary. If you're still waiting for your first secretary, expect to carry the administrative load. Hopefully, you won't have to wait eighteen years!

12. Can I use volunteers to help with administrative tasks?

Yes. Many times adults will come to you to work in your program, but they aren't comfortable teaching. They offer to type, bake, or do whatever else needs to be done. I ask if they're available during the day. If they are, I find out if they would come to the office and help during peak busy periods or once a week. These volunteers usually enjoy this work and feel needed in the program, while saving me many hours of paperwork.

13. How can we avoid misusing the copy machine in our program?

The copy machine has become a very popular tool in our ministry. And although it is a great aid, it can be overused and misused. There's always the temptation to violate copyrights. It's easy to rationalize our need to copy materials rather than purchase extra books because of our limited budgets. In addition to being morally wrong, we are giving the wrong message to our catechists and students when we reproduce copyright materials. If there are handouts with important information for the family, make enough copies to give to the oldest child in the family rather than to every child in the program. If you feel that some teachers are continually asking for copies to be made, you might want to keep a monthly log of copies made. The use of copies could be a topic at a teachers' meeting, with input from the group on the effective use of copies, such as encouraging creativity rather than using ready-made handouts which require copying.

14. How can I get information to the families of the children in the program?

My first source is the parish bulletin. I realize that in every parish there are those who religiously read the weekly bulletin as well as those who never look at it. But I've found that it's a good vehicle to keep the entire parish aware of what's going on in the religious education program. And for those "faithful readers" it's a good reminder of the upcoming week's activities. Realizing that *everyone* doesn't use it for a weekly check, it's good to use other media for reminding our families of meetings, classes, etc. This can involve placing posters on the bulletin board outside of the church, having pulpit announcements for very special reminders, and sending letters or flyers home through the children. However, mailing works best when it's important that the message get through.

15. What materials should I include in my annual budget for administration needs?

This will depend on how your annual budget is set up. Some parishes include secretarial needs for the entire parish under one heading; others subdivide for the different programs. But whether you share the allotted budget or itemize your own, you'll basically be looking at the following items for this account:

☐ duplicating paper—reams of white and colored stock
☐ construction paper—packages of 9 x 12, 12 x 18, 18 x 36, etc.
☐ stationery with parish heading, with matching envelopes

- [ ] typewriter supplies: ribbons, erasing materials, paper
- [ ] computer printer supplies: software, paper, labels, ribbons
- [ ] general office supplies: pencils, pens, tape, staplers

16. Since we have a budget, I like to know how much money I've used and what's available for spending. Is there a simple bookkeeping procedure I can use to keep me informed?

I've used an accounting notebook to keep a record of my expenses as well as my income for the program. Each month I set up the page, using the left side for money coming in, and the right side for expenses incurred. As bills come in, I mark the date, the item purchased, and the amount. When it is paid, I record the date of payment. In parishes using a code for their budget, you'll want to also include this information on your sheet. With the advent of the computer, many DREs are keeping their accounts on software. There are programs designed for this. They'll save you hours of bookkeeping time.

17. Most programs charge a registration fee each year. When is the best time to collect this fee?

Because there is such a demand for money each school year in September, I like to collect the religious education fee in the spring. When families pre-register for the coming year, they make their payment. If money is a problem, they have the option of making a partial payment. I have found most families like this plan for payment. One year we separated our fees. We charged a family registration fee in the spring to cover administrative needs. When the program began the students paid a book fee to cover the cost of the books they would use and keep. No one wants money to stand in the way of providing religious education, but we must be realistic about the financial demands of providing a program. And we should not apologize for charging a fee to offset the cost.

18. I would like to use children's church envelopes in our program. How can I do this?

If your program wants the children to use offering envelopes, you can order these in bulk quantities from church supply catalogues. Using envelopes can teach children the importance and value of giving to the church in a tangible way. When you have a separate liturgy or liturgy of the word, you'll want to include a collection of the offering as well as a presentation of these gifts. If the children are part of the adult community they should be encouraged to put their offering envelope in the baskets when their parents do so. This will help prepare them for understanding stewardship.

19. Should the administrative personnel be responsible for getting substitutes when teachers call in to say they can't be there for class?

I have always had the teachers get their own substitutes when they know they will not be there for their class. In my early years as a DRE I had the teachers call me or the office when they needed a replacement. I found that this was one of my biggest headaches, and I knew there had to be a better way. One solution to the problem was having two teachers for each classroom. If one had to cancel, the other could take over the class. But now I have an even better solution. Teachers are responsible to get their own substitutes. They are encouraged to take care of this weeks ahead of time. In the case of sudden illness, they should first try to get help from the substitute list. If they are unsuccessful, they should call the office—but this should be the exception, not the rule.

20. How can the administrator be of assistance to the teachers?

They can be called upon to provide class lists, schedules for classes, and teachers' and substitute teachers' names, addresses, and telephone numbers. They can also help teachers by making copies for them—within reason—and providing supplies for their classrooms. However, it's important for the DRE to see that the administrator's services are not abused or taken for granted.

8
Children's Programs
How To Make Them Easier

DREs came into being because of children—the need to give them theology and values. With the demise of the parochial school, we experienced the emergence of the CCD program. And our religious education programs have focused on children ever since. However, today our parishes have grown, and our need for children's programs and all it takes to coordinate them demands professionalism. Although children are only one of the groups you work with, they are usually the largest. Meeting the needs of the children in your parish is the focus of this chapter.

1. Are we confusing parishioners when we call our programs for children RE instead of CCD?

CCD originally stood for Confraternity of Christian Doctrine. Although many knew that CCD meant catechism classes, few knew what the initials meant. Today it's much easier to understand that RE stands for religious education. In reality both refer to the same thing—classes for children not attending parochial school. As a DRE you can educate your parishioners by using RE rather than CCD. However you may find that it's hard to break old habits.

2. Should children attend religious education classes even though they are attending the Catholic school?

It depends. If your religious education program is using the same curriculum as the parochial school, it would be repetitive to attend both. However, some programs follow a different syllabus and encourage children in both parochial and public schools to attend classes. You do have the perfect opportunity to bring these two groups together in your sacramental preparation classes and special celebrations.

3. My parish has an abundance of young families with pre-school children. How can I provide for them?

If at all possible, set up and staff pre-school classes. The pre-school program can be one of the most rewarding areas in your children's program. Just watching the children ages three to five in their classroom should convince any DRE of their value. If you can schedule their classes during Mass times, you provide an added incentive for families to enroll their young children. Today most pre-schoolers are already attending classes during the week, and are enthusiastic about being a part of the parish religious education program.

4. I am trying to decide between Sunday religious education classes and classes after school. Are there any problems in having religious education classes after school during the week?

For years I worked as a catechist in religious education classes after school. I remember how hard it was to keep the children's attention. They had just spent the whole day at school, and now they were asked to come for *one more hour.* There were also other circumstances—after school activities such as scouts and sports, and parents who worked outside the home—that made it difficult for children to attend classes scheduled at this hour.

5. I can't decide whether to schedule my classes on Saturday or Sunday morning. What are the pros and cons of each?

On Saturday morning the parish facilities are relatively free for religion classes. You won't have to adjust your schedule to the parish Mass schedule or compete with the heavy traffic. On the other hand, many families look forward to that one day of the week

---

ADAPTING TO THE LOCAL SITUATION

All the reasons for having programs scheduled on Saturdays or Sundays will carry no weight if you find yourself working in certain areas of the country—areas where weekends are spent away from the parish community. This could be in the west where skiing is a family sport, or in the lake districts where boating and lakeside activities draw the families from the weekday scene, or a similar place where the community is transient.

If you are working in a parish which disappears on weekends, the last thing you want to do is schedule classes during that time. It's important to adapt to your locale. Choose the time and place for classes that blends into the lifestyle of your people. If you do, your people will appreciate your sensitivity to their needs and participate in the programs you offer.

---

they don't have to get up early—for school, work, or church. Further, if your children are involved in soccer or other sports, Saturday morning is usually "game time." On Sunday morning, you need to be concerned with your class times and how they affect the regular Mass schedule, parish activities, and, of course, the traffic problem. On the positive side, Sundays for most families are already set aside for church-going. Religion classes held near the church and coordinated with the different Masses will make it easier for parents to bring children to class. Some parishes also schedule adult classes at the same time for parents. I've always preferred the Sunday morning schedule. And I've found that the majority of families prefer this time. As a DRE you should look at *your local situation*—the pros and cons—before you schedule class times.

6. I'd like to set up a schedule of classes for the year. Are there any directives on how often classes should meet?

Most programs are set up on a weekly basis, from September to May. But there are other options. Classes can be twice a month, or even once a month, meeting for a longer period of time. The number of *hours* you meet will be about the same no matter what schedule you decide upon. Many times your schedule will be dictated by your curriculum. Once you decide your schedule, you'll want to distribute copies of it to all the families at the beginning of each school year.

7. How long should a class period be for elementary school children?

Again, this will depend on how often you meet. You'll want at least *an hour* for a class that meets weekly. Most lesson plans are organized on an hour schedule. Since taking attendance and closing class take additional time, you'll want to add a few minutes— scheduling your class for more than an hour. If you're meeting only twice a month, then your class time will be longer. And if you're on a monthly time frame, you're looking at a unique schedule of three hours divided into short rotating classes.

8. Is it wise to follow the school year calendar in scheduling religious education classes?

Family calendars are built around the school calendar, and your religious education program should fit into this same calendar. That's why I like to start in September when everyone's eager to start school—and religious education. It's smart to refer to the school calendar so that you don't schedule conflicting events in religious education. As the spring brings heavy social demands, it's time to ease up on class sessions. And just as the teachers take a summer break, your catechists will also be ready for time off.

(In this area use theme logo from catechetical Sunday for year as heading.)

ADD NAME OF PARISH AND YEAR

SCHEDULE OF CLASSES

Sept. 11 - Classes Begin
18 - Class
25 - Class

Oct. 2 - *Oktoberfest*
(Free)
9 - Class
16 - Class
23 - Class

Nov. 6 - Class
13 - Class
20 - Class
27 - *Thanksgiving*
(Free)

Dec. 4 - Class
11 - Class
18 - Class
25 - *Christmas*
(Free)

Jan. 1 - *New Year's Day*
(Free)
8 - Class
15 - Class
22 - Class

Feb. 5 - Class
12 - Class
19 - *Washington's B'day*
(Free)
26 - Class

March 5 - Class
12 - Class
19 - Class
26 - *Easter (Free)*

April 2 - Class
9 - Class
16 - Class
23 - Final Class
30 - Closing Liturgy

May 6 & 13 -
Celebration of
First Eucharist

June 12–22 -
Summer Program

9. Can I plan any free days for religious education during the year?

I like to schedule at least one free Sunday each month. This gives not only the children and families time off, but also all your teachers and workers. Some of these free Sundays are the holiday weekends that will always be free, such as Thanksgiving weekend, Christmas vacation, and Easter. But others are scheduled to fit the parish needs, or the teachers' needs for a break.

10. How can I decide what materials to use for children in the elementary program?

There are a variety of materials to choose from in setting up your elementary program. Many times when you begin working in a parish, your materials have already been ordered. In this case, you'll have no decision making for a year. However, as a DRE you should have a voice in future materials for your programs. Publishers are more than happy to send you samples of their product. You should work together with your religious education board (if you have one) in deciding which materials will help attain your goals. Once this is decided, contact the publisher. Sometimes they'll even provide a workshop on using their materials.

11. Are there any specific materials for pre-schoolers?

It's not unusual for parents to think that pre-school during liturgies is just a babysitting service. They are surprised when I show them an organized curriculum with manuals, textbooks and handouts for their children. With the new emphasis on pre-school education, publishers have responded with attractive and interesting books for the little ones. I recommend that you look over the different programs available and select the one that fits your parish needs. Some DREs try to keep costs down by creating their own materials. In reality their time and energy are worth more than the cost of books. Parents don't mind paying a fee when they see you're using it for good materials.

12. What is the advantage of the children keeping their books at the end of the year?

Many teachers prefer that the children keep their textbooks in the room during the year. They find that if the children take them home each week, they won't return for the next lesson. Home study books and take home sheets are used for getting the message of the lesson home. If children are allowed to keep their books, they can get into the home at the end of the year. During the summer months, when classes are not in session, they can be used for review. Many children like to have their books as a keepsake. I know that my own children have kept their religion books over the years when they've freely tossed out other workbooks.

13. How can I best use AV materials in the children's program?

Our children live in a multimedia world. We need to take advantage of the numerous filmstrips, movies, and video cassettes available to us. The little ones—pre-school and primary grades—never tire of stories on the screen. As children move beyond the primary grades, they'll begin resisting the message of filmstrips, but will be open to movies and videos. There are a few basic rules I try to adhere to in using AVs. (Note sidebar on using AV materials.)

14. Should a student ever be retained in the same grade?

If a child is retained in regular school, I encourage the parents to retain their child in religious education. This is not because the child has not passed RE, but rather to keep the student with the same group he or she is with during the week. And most families are comfortable with this policy. Generally, however, all children move into the next grade at the end of the year in the religious education programs unless a parent requests otherwise.

15. What can I tell parents who complain that their children don't want to come to class?

I usually tell them that their children are *normal*—especially if we're talking about youngsters over nine years of age. They probably complain about going to school during the week too. Many times it's the "in thing" not to want to go to RE or church, and children are just responding to their peers. It's interesting to listen to children talk about their classes. They'll leave a classroom all excited, and by the time they reach their parents they've changed moods. We need to support parents and show them it's worthwhile for their child to be attending classes. And after we've done our best, we can accept the negativism, knowing that it's not a completely honest evaluation of their true feelings.

16. Parents often wonder if their children will learn catechism questions as they did. Does this fit into our programs?

If there's anything we can boast of in the pre-Vatican church, it was our memorization of the catechism. One of the concerns of the post-Vatican Church is our children's inability to answer basic questions about their faith. However, we are beginning to see a return of "answers to be learned" in religion texts. The difference between these questions and our "Baltimore questions" is that they are presented after the lesson as a summary of truths and not as an entity unto themselves. I don't think it's too much to ask our students to memorize as a reinforcement to learning, as long as it is done within reason.

17. What's the secret to keep children in the intermediate grades (4-6) coming to weekly classes?

I've found that the secret is having catechists who understand children at this age—catechists who make classes interesting and keep the children involved. There is a big change in children beginning with Grade 4. The influence of the peer group and the questioning of values affects their attitude about coming to classes. They aren't going to be satisfied with reading the lesson and doing a related activity. The more variety and surprises you can build into their classes, the more they'll want to come—and the more they'll learn.

18. How strict should I be about frequent absenteeism?

You need to be very definite about your policy on attendance and enforce it at all levels. If you're meeting weekly, it's a good idea to have children bring excuses the week they return to class. I ask the individual teachers to follow up on absentees, having them call students after they've missed twice to see if there's a problem. This is one way to show we care about the children we teach, and it may reveal a family situation we are unaware of. Try to be sensitive to families where children spend alternate weekends with each parent. The children should not be made to feel guilty about something beyond their control. Most parents are grateful for support we can give them in these situations.

19. How can I handle the problems that arise because of using someone else's facilities for our religious education classes?

This is one of those questions that is hard to answer in a few sentences. In fact, I've written an entire chapter on this subject. (See *Through the Year with the DRE*, "Sharing the Territory.") In our position as a DRE we need to communicate openly and honestly with others who use the same facilities. There will always be problems! However, if you have a positive and supportive attitude, rather than a defensive one, you'll be able to work them out. At the same time, help your catechists and students to develop this same attitude—even when things get "messy."

20. My catechists complain that we have the children for only an hour each week. How can that short session make a difference in their lives?

I've often reminded my catechists that they are there to help the parents in forming values for the children. In that one hour they can only *reinforce* what is being done in the home. The children who come to us can be shown how they are living their faith. We can send home "parent pages" as a tangible way for children and parents to share. Hopefully we will bridge what is taught in the classroom with what is being lived within the home.

9

Youth Ministry
Bring In the Teens!

Working with teenagers is one of the biggest challenges for any DRE. To have a competent youth coordinator is a great blessing. More and more parishes are aware of this need and are hiring either part-time or full-time youth coordinators. For too long we have been satisfied to have scheduled classes for the teens with an occasional retreat and social gathering. Today the church must do more or we will lose our young people. Although we can't cover all aspects of this ministry in this chapter, let's look at some important areas the DRE should consider.

1. I have been asked to assist in the hiring of a parish youth coordinator. What qualities should I look for in this person?

The most important quality for a youth coordinator is someone who not only understands teens but *likes* them! Teenagers can sense immediately if an adult really wants to be with them or is just putting in hours. Other qualities to look for are current knowledge of theology, educational experience with teens, an understanding of group dynamics, administrative skills, and the ability to work with teens in a mature manner.

2. How can I provide for the needs of the youth of my parish when we're not able to hire a youth coordinator?

If you're not able to hire a coordinator, you'll want to look for a person or a couple willing to work with you as a volunteer youth coordinator. Of course you won't have the luxury of a full-time helper, but at least there will be someone who can help in a part-time capacity. And maybe you'll eventually be able to move this person into a paid position. Meanwhile you will be able to have this person assist you in scheduling classes for the teens, planning retreats, and doing some of the necessary administrative work. Since you're depending on volunteers, you might want to add another person to coordinate just social activities.

3. I want to find the best catechists for the teens. What qualities should I look for in my search?

Just as the youth coordinator should like teens, so too should the catechists who are working with this group. I've found that couples working together with a group of teens make a good combination. Their complementary qualities enhance the relationship they can have with teenagers. You'll want to be aware of adults who are going to "instruct them properly." These folks can turn off this age group quickly. Teens don't want to be preached at by someone who is "all-wise." They are looking for someone who cares about them and their needs. This someone will instruct more by example than any words.

4. How can I schedule classes to fit into the teens' already overcrowded calendars?

Before scheduling classes talk to the teens who will be participating in your program. They'll be honest about scheduling to avoid conflict with school programs and activities. An hour or two one night a week is usually all you'll get for religious activities, so make the best of it. If your facilities allow you to schedule more than one night for the teens, give *them* the option of selecting the best night. I've often heard teens voice their preference for Sunday morning because the rest of their family is involved in religious education at that time. They say it doesn't infringe on homework time or social activities. Scheduling classes and activities is one area you don't want to handle until you hear from the teens.

5. Do I have any options in scheduling my teen program?

Yes, but before you begin any type of programming for your parish, find out what programs have worked in the past and which haven't—why some were successful and others were not. Just as it was necessary to talk to the teens about the best times for classes, it's a good idea to meet with the teens to discuss options for class scheduling. Combine your expertise with their experience to work out the best formula for programs. If they've been meeting once a month for years, it may be a good time to shift gears and look at a new approach. Similarly, if they've had weekly classes forever, they'll welcome a change. What's best for one parish is not necessarily best for another. Tailor your program to fit the particular needs of the teens in your parish.

6. I'm hearing that more parishes are using the modular system. How does this system work?

The modular system is organized into six-week units dividing the classes according to themes. Students sign up for one class each

---

THE MODULAR SYSTEM

This system for scheduling classes can be used in both junior and senior high programs. Classes are listed under themes. Teens should sign up for classes themselves. A record is kept of all classes attended in order to guide the teens in selecting classes under all of the class themes.

Junior High Themes:
Church • Jesus and the Gospel Message • Personal Growth • Relationships • Morality and Moral Decision Making • Service • Sexuality

Senior High Themes:
Faith and Identity • Gospels • Hebrew Scripture • Jesus • Justice and Peace • Love and Lifestyles • Morality • Paul and His Letters • Prayer and Worship

period under a specific theme. The following period they register for a class under another theme. Over the years their classes will cover all the themes, providing variety and balance to their religious education curriculum. (Note the modular plan outlined in this chapter.) This system is popular with youth who want to make their own class selections. Further, because classes change every six weeks, the interest of the students is maintained.

7. I'd like to organize our youth program to include both formal and informal sessions. Is this possible?

It's not only possible, but today it's strongly recommended that we organize a total youth program in our parishes. For too long we have separated formal classes from social gatherings of the teens. We put the emphasis on attending classes, limiting our focus of religious education. Today we want to expand our approach to include both formal and informal learning situations. This means scheduling classes and lecture series, inviting guest speakers for formal learning situations, and organizing retreats, service projects, and fellowship evenings as opportunities for informal learning to take place. Students are encouraged to participate in both types of learning situations throughout their teenage years.

8. Can some type of "credit" system be set up for our youth religious education program?

Yes, giving credit for religious education courses is becoming quite popular today. It gives an added motivation to the teens to attend all the classes in a given course because credit is *only* given for *full participation.* By applying credits it gives them a sense of fulfillment when each course is completed. Be sure to determine ahead of time how credits will be distributed for the various programs. The amount of credit for a retreat weekend would be considerably more than that given for attending an evening lecture. I've known parishes where credits were the basis of readiness for the confirmation program. However, with sacramental preparation we must be sensitive to each candidate's situation.

9. Are there some important factors I should keep in mind as I schedule retreats for teens?

Teenagers' retreats are one of the best opportunities for young people to grow in their understanding of their faith. Retreats are not something we add onto the curriculum. They are at the *heart* of a good program. And because of this, it's helpful to schedule several retreats throughout the year. Again, we must be aware of busy calendars and try not to conflict with events at the local high schools. If you're experienced in working with teens, you'll know this isn't easy. Since they extend over a full weekend—Friday evening to Sunday afternoon—you'll be asking for a real commitment from both the teens and the adults who will be participating. But it's worth it! Take advantage of the numerous books on the market to help you plan your retreats.

10. Whom should I call upon to help me plan and organize a retreat?

Without question, consult your adult catechists who are working with the teens. Since these are the people who already know the teenagers, they should be the first adults we invite to help plan a retreat. They've already given of their time and can relate to the teens in a faith-sharing environment. However, don't limit your retreat team to this group. Since some teachers aren't interested or able to do retreat work, call on other adults for help. You will need presenters, cooks, chaperones, and drivers in order to take care of the many facets of the retreat. The more adults we can get involved in these weekends, the better. For these are the times we have the best opportunity to get to know our teenagers.

11. Should I get the teens involved in planning their retreats?

We should not only get them involved in planning, but in some instances train them to actually present part of the retreat. Of course, this isn't something you do the first time you schedule a retreat. Only after you get to know your teens, identify the leaders, and experience a retreat can you properly draw upon their talents. This is an excellent opportunity for peer ministry. We should move from planning the retreat alone, to where we call upon both the adults and teens to assist us in setting up the retreat. When this group is comfortable in planning, it can begin delegating part of the retreat to the teens. It's when they reach this final phase that you must be ready to deal with the outcome. It will have a few rough edges, but that's how we learn.

12. I'll be working with the sacrament of confirmation. Are there any guidelines for preparation for this sacrament?

The big question that we've wrestled with for years has been at what age should we prepare for confirmation. We've seen this sacrament move from preparation during the sixth grade to preparation during senior high, with many variations in between. Theologians aren't much help. They tell us that there is no right age and that since it is one of the sacraments of initiation it belongs with baptism. There's even talk of moving it back to the earlier years again. But for now we are working with it during the high school years, so let's consider preparation for that age group. First of all, there have been no long-standing guidelines. Many dioceses and deaneries have taken this task to heart and developed guidelines for their area. The general characteristics are a two-year preparation program with three phases—classroom study, service projects, and periods of prayer and renewal. There is also an involvement of the entire parish community as the teens go through the stages of preparation where rites are included in the Sunday liturgy. However, each parish must decide on its particular preparation program and materials to be used.

13. Is confirmation like a graduation from the religious education program?

Absolutely not! But unfortunately many teens feel that this is *exactly* what it is. They have attended classes for years, and as they approach the end of their high school years they will be confirmed and become graduates of RE. Not only do the teens believe this, but their parents are saying the very same thing. For most of them, the next sacrament they will receive will be matrimony, and that's the next time they'll be appearing at the church office to sign up for classes. Because we are a strong sacramental church we have built our need for instructions around preparation for the sacraments. And it will be a long slow process to change this concept.

14. Why should we encourage projects involving our teens in service toward the community?

Teenagers expend much of their energy on their own needs. To an outsider they can appear to be very selfish. But this is a changing period in their lives, and they use lots of energy just trying to understand what's happening in their world. We can channel some of this energy by providing opportunities for them to reach out to others. There are endless ways they can serve both within and beyond the parish, such as working in the parish nursery, helping with pre-school classes, visiting the elderly and writing letters for them, etc. (Note the section on gift-giving for an example of service.) And hopefully after they've experienced the joy in serving others, they may want to continue helping in projects and programs.

GIVING TREE PROJECT

This project gets teens involved in giving to the elderly and the infirm at the neighborhood nursing homes located within the parish.

1. Go to the nursing homes within the parish and explain this project to the director. If they decide to participate ask for the names of the residents who live in the home. You can ask them to specify a gift they would like for Christmas, placing their name and gift they would like on a small card.
2. Have the teens set up the Christmas "giving tree" in the church. Most churches have guidelines on where they want the tree situated. Place the cards in envelopes and tie them to the tree with ribbons.
3. Invite parishioners to take a card and buy the gift requested. If there is no gift specified, buy a gift you think the person would like.
4. Wrap the gift, put the person's name on it, and place it under the tree before the designated date (usually about a week before Christmas).
5. Teens gather to deliver gifts about a week before Christmas. Sometimes caroling accompanies the delivering of gifts.

15. Should the teens raise funds to carry on their activities?

We all know how money is necessary for even our charitable works. Yet there is often a problem of how to obtain this money. The parish budget takes care of materials for classes. But there are always those extra expenses—money for paying the chaperones' admission to an activity, for sending greetings to residents in the home for the aged, for refreshments during fellowship evenings, etc. In some parishes the youth are allotted a certain amount for service projects, but when this is not covered they should devise novel ways to earn it. Car washes, bake sales, and raffle tickets are good ideas if they are not overdone. Working together on fund-raisers can be helpful in building community and can give the teens a sense of pride. So don't discourage the teens from rolling up their sleeves and earning a few dollars for their projects. But be careful. You don't want fund-raisers to be the one thing your program is noted for. It should be the charitable results of their fund-raisers that matter!

16. How can I offer programs where teens and parents can come together to learn?

This is another challenge to you as coordinator of the youth—bridging the gap between parents and teens! There are two types of parent programs that I've seen work well at this level. The first is offering courses for parents while you're having classes for the teens. Offer a course on understanding adolescence and you're guaranteed an audience. However, don't limit your curriculum to this area. Courses on Vatican II theology, morality, and scripture are also appealing. Coordinate your break times and encourage teens and adults to mingle. Even though most of the teens will cluster together, some will dare to talk with the adults. Another approach to parent programs is offering classes where teens and adults attend the same lecture and then separate into small groups for discussion. This has worked well in the new sex education programs. If we can do anything to improve parent-teen relationships in our programs, we will be responding to a great need for both groups.

17. How can I use the teens' talents in working with the children of our parish?

Teens are a welcome addition to any pre-school program. They can also assist in the primary grades. Although many teens prefer to assist the teacher, there are those who are comfortable teaching the little ones, especially pre-schoolers. They have the patience and understanding needed to cope with the demands of the young children. I always encourage the youth to help in the summer program. For many it's their first experience of "giving" as teachers in contrast to "receiving" as students. They are also helpful in the nursery which combines playing and teaching as well as caring for the needs of infants and toddlers.

18. What ages are we including when we say "youth program"?

It varies. In the past youth program meant high school program. Now we are seeing this program expand to include the pre-teens. This would include either the middle school students or junior high students—depending on the school system in your area. Since their needs aren't exactly the same as the older teenagers, you'll want to structure your program to accommodate this. You may wish to call the pre-teens program "Youth Prep" and the high schoolers "Youth." Both groups would be under the youth coordinator and considered a part of the parish youth ministry program.

19. Shouldn't I also include the "young adults" in our youth ministry program?

Yes, if possible this group between the ages of eighteen and twenty-one should be brought into our youth ministry network. All too often these are the forgotten group. They've graduated from high school and moved on—but not always away. Although a large number of graduates go away for their college years, there are many who either attend the local college or begin a job in the local community. They remain at home and continue to participate in the liturgical life of the parish. But what do we offer them in our religious education program? Many parishes have a social group for this age, but this is only taking care of one of their needs. We might begin by gathering some members of this age group at the church to talk about their needs. Hopefully this will lead to setting up programs to meet those needs. We cannot ignore our young adults if we are serving the *total* parish community.

20. How can I ever meet so wide a range of needs for the youth by myself?

You can't, unless you are some type of a super-being. You'll soon burn out if you try to do it alone. You must be honest and accept your limitations. You'll need *help* to carry out the tasks before you. That's when you should look to your faith community. If your funds are limited and you can't hire help, search for good volunteers and delegate. Use the members of your religious education board in the youth interest group for input, planning and implementation of programs.

10
Adult Education
We're Never Too Old To Learn

Adult education is not a new concept in our church. But since Vatican II there has been an increased awareness of a need for ongoing education programs. Some parishes can boast of successful adult education programs where large numbers attend weekly lectures and scheduled classes. However, many parishes continue to struggle to provide adult programs. Who is responsible for the adult education program? Is it the pastor, the DRE, the religious education board, or some other organization? As a DRE you'll be either directly or indirectly responsible for what's happening in adult education. In this chapter, we will look at the many aspects of adult education.

1. Why should I be concerned with providing adult education programs today?

So much has changed in our church in the last twenty-five years. Most adult Catholics will admit that. At the same time they're hesitant to sign up for a class to find out about these changes. Many feel they will show their ignorance in a group setting. And yet, if you listen to their comments, you'll hear a crying need for classes or lectures on theological updating. We are challenged to offer these opportunities in a non-threatening way. If we put our energies into teaching the children and ignore their parents and the adults of the parish, we're being unfair to both groups.

2. How should the pastor be involved in the adult education program in the parish?

The pastor should be concerned with meeting the needs of his people. As head of the community he leads them in prayer and in ways that will deepen their faith life. Adult education is a prime concern because we are talking about the total person's growth. The pastor should work with you and the religious education board in planning adult education classes. Some pastors have extensive theological backgrounds and are anxious to teach classes for adults on a regular basis or when the need arises. Others prefer to delegate this task to others—deacons, adult education teachers, parish professionals—giving their support to these groups.

3. I'm just not comfortable working in adult education. Whom can I turn to for help in setting up programs for adults?

If your parish has an adult education coordinator, count yourself blessed. With the onset of pastoral associates, many of whom are women, we are experiencing another professional person to take on the responsibility of adult education in the parish. Should your situation lack either of these positions, you can turn to your religious education board. This group of parishioners are there to support you and provide ways to enhance your education program. If you are missing all of the above, your first task is to recruit a volunteer or two to help you coordinate the adult education programs in your parish. You don't have to tackle this job alone!

4. Is this an area where deacons can help?

I would hope so. Most have relatively recent theological training. However, since most deacons are already helping parishes on a voluntary basis, you have to be sensitive to the demands you make of them. If you are in a situation where one of your deacons has a keen insight into the adult education needs of the community, you can turn to him for help in setting up programs. By all means you'll want to use your deacons in implementing and providing adult education classes in theology updating, sacramental preparation, and other areas of concern in your parish.

5. I've heard it said that the sacramental preparation program for parents can open the door for further adult education. How does it do this?

I have found that many times adults are not comfortable signing up for regular adult education classes in theology. They feel they have to know something about theology before they join a class. However, they are willing to attend the required parent classes in order to have their children receive the sacraments. And once they begin coming to these classes, they start asking for further opportunities to increase their understanding of the faith.

6. Adult education covers all ages from college to senior citizens. How can I address these different age groups?

Basic courses in scripture, moral theology, and sacraments are not limited to one age group—all adults should welcome the opportunity for instruction in all these areas. However, there are specific needs for young adults which we need to be aware of. If you can get a small group of young adults to form a committee to pursue the needs of this group, you're off to a good start. The same is true of any other groups, such as senior citizens. We can study the needs of the elderly, but it's much better to work hand in hand with them. There is an emphasis on peer ministry in the church today—this applies to adult education too.

7. What would you say is different in our approach to adult education today?

To put it simply, it's on formation rather than information. In the past our major concern was content—learning doctrine. Today we are more wholistic in our approach to adult education—it's not only a head trip. Although there is a need for good theology, we must be more concerned with integrating it into our daily life. We did a great job on imparting *knowledge* in the past. Just ask anyone over forty a question from the Baltimore Catechism. The true test is whether those truths really changed our lives.

8. What should I include in my budget for adult education?

If you want to know where your parish places its priorities, take a look at its last year's budget. Where did you spend your money? We say we want good adult religious education. Do we budget accordingly? We need to consider the cost of stipends for professional speakers, rentals for video materials and 16mm films, and manuals and books for classes. Good materials cost money, but many times these are one time only expenses. Remember, some of these expenses will be reimbursed through fees for attendance at lectures or film series and book sales. And then there is the cost for conventions, workshops, etc. for the teachers. Certainly educating our teachers opens the way to further education for our parish community.

9. I feel that I am already doing adult education in the total religious education program. How can I highlight this fact?

I recall reading an article on the many ways DREs are providing adult education, yet they aren't given credit for having *any* adult education program. They are reaching adults through their children's programs—with parenting classes and sacramental preparation classes, and through the in-service classes for the catechists. These classes are more than practicum sessions; they contain good theology too. When we advertise our adult education programs for the year, we should include these classes. In fact it's a good idea to open these sessions to all adults in the parish, not only the parents and catechists.

10. Why is publicity so important in setting up adult religious education programs?

We have a good product—but somehow we don't always market it well. If we rely on bulletin and pulpit announcements, we are limiting our audience. Although there have never been any statistics on the percentage of families who actually read the bulletin, as a DRE you know that many *do not*. We'll go into some practical points on publicity in the chapter devoted to this. Let it suffice to say that we cannot overdo publicizing our programs. You don't want to hear, "I would have liked to attend that adult education class, but I *never heard* anything about it."

11. There is a resurgence of interest by adults in studying the Bible. How can I respond to that need?

For years Catholics were not encouraged to study the Bible. Many felt that you needed to be a scripture scholar in order to teach others. Ironically those who were interested in doing serious studies would join one of the Christian or non-denominational church study groups. But this is changing. Catholic parishes are now offering opportunities to study scripture. We need to respond to this need by providing some form of scripture study program—either through lectures and classes or small discussion groups.

12. How do I know which scripture program is best for the parish?

There are many scripture programs to choose from today. If you are setting up a new program, check out the different publications before you make a decision. You might want to attend programs in neighboring parishes for a better understanding of the various approaches. If you have some adults who are interested in working with you, all the better. Form a committee to evaluate and order materials, to set up a schedule, and to publicize your new program.

13. Are Bible study groups the same as faith sharing groups?

Not always. With Bible study groups, scripture is the focus for study, interpretation, and application. Many times the emphasis is on the scriptural meaning rather than its application. However, it's when making the connection between scripture and our daily lives that the study becomes more than an academic exercise . . . it becomes an experience in faith sharing. And although scripture is the best source for faith sharing, other materials can also be used for this process . . . such as texts on theology, morality, and current topics in the church. With the movement toward small faith communities, we are observing a parallel move toward faith sharing groups.

14. Are there any adult education programs that have a reputation for being successful?

I have found that programs that involve the whole parish and are based on a renewal effort are the most successful. This is a change from the structured approach of scheduling a series of classes or lectures and having registration. It is a more widespread approach. If you decide to implement a program of this type, there are months of homework in preparation before it is opened to the parish at large. You need good volunteers to form your core group. This group, together with the pastoral team, will lay the groundwork for an adult program that can reach into almost every home in your parish. There will always be those who will reject anything that is offered. These renewal programs are based on a long term schedule and aim at offering a total adult program of prayer, study, and fellowship. I highly recommend this type of adult education. It's worth the effort!

15. Why should I use films and video tapes in adult education?

There is no question about the fact we are living in an age of visual media. Our religious education programs would be missing a valuable tool if we ignored the market of films and videos. There are parenting series, marriage related series, and issues of the day, to only name a few. We can ill afford to hire all these experts for our parish. Yet they are available to us through exciting videos and films. If you decide to schedule a particular series, make sure you publicize it well and prepare adults to present the materials. Even though your main presentation will be with the media, you'll want someone to welcome the people, prepare them for the presentation, and follow it up with discussions.

THE VALUE OF VIDEOS

1. Provide professional speakers and programs.
2. Have up-to-date materials on all subject areas.
3. Appeal to all types of adult groups.
4. Can be set up for either small or large groups.
5. Have been produced in series for study purposes.
6. Are readily available through rental centers from church offices or commercial video rentals.
7. Can be purchased at reasonable costs for future use.
8. Can be checked out of parish for make-up classes.
9. Are a source of adult education that can be used in the home environment.
10. Can be used for catechist inservice or enrichment.

---

16. Why should I consider scheduling home study discussion groups in the parish?

There is something more intimate about faith sharing done in the comfort of someone's living room. Usually couples who gather together already know each other to some degree. This makes communication and sharing easier. However, when there is a familiarity, the facilitator has an added challenge of making sure the group keeps with the topic under discussion. Home discussion groups can be set up using the subdivisions of the parish as a guide, providing an opportunity for neighboring parishioners to get to know each other. By using materials already arranged for home study, you are bringing adult education into the homes in a practical and non-threatening way. Again, you'll want to train your leaders before you launch into a full home study program.

17. How do I know whom to select to facilitate these sharing-discussion groups?

Once you have set up your divisions and you know what families will be included in each area, you're ready to search for your facilitators. Depending on the size of your parish, this task can be relatively easy or extremely difficult. Some adults are more comfortable in a leadership role than others. It's important to stress the facilitator's role as just that—one of *facilitating*, not teaching, manipulating, or dominating the group.

18. Are there any special groups we should be ministering to in our adult education programs?

If we are reaching out to all members of our parish, we should be including programs for those who are somewhat alienated or hurting—the divorced and separated, the single parents, young adults who aren't married, those who have lost a loved one through death, etc. These adults need support and help in their particular situations. If the church can't come to their need through support and discussion groups, reaching out in a loving way, whom can they turn to?

19. As a DRE I don't feel qualified to work with the special groups of adults such as the divorced and separated, single parents, etc. What can I do to meet their needs?

All DREs have areas in which they feel more comfortable than others. For some it's working with the children, while others get more satisfaction working with the adult community. In our role as a DRE we can't expect to be experts in all areas, but we can search for the experts. This is especially true when working with those "hurting" members of our community. If you don't find anyone in your own parish, look beyond it to the neighboring parishes or the diocesan office. Many times support groups can be formed to include more than one parish in an area.

20. When should I begin planning for guest lecturer programs?

You need to plan this type of program at least several months in advance in order to recruit good speakers. However, I'd strongly recommend that you plan your speakers for the coming year during the summer months. If you're using good speakers, they'll be in demand. And like so many commitments, it's a first-come, first-served situation.

11
Family-Centered Programs
The Family That Stays Together . . .

The church has been involved in family life since its establishment. And the 1980s became the decade of the family. Yet ironically there are numerous instances of church involvement being a source of division rather than of strength for the family. The constant demands on different family members of meetings, committees, and volunteer work can split up families, leaving little time for each other at home. The emergence of a family life committee was a move in the right direction in supporting the family. Programs were established in parishes for the entire family, and educational materials were published using a family religious education approach. Thus the family was again given a priority in parish life. How the DRE supports families and family-centered programs is the subject of this chapter.

1. I've heard about parishes that have family-centered programming. What is it?

Programs that include all the members of the family and are directed toward the family are called family-centered programs. They have always been a part of parish life; however, they may have been called by a different name. Activities such as parish picnics, potluck suppers, and annual festivals are examples. As DREs we need to look at these types of activities and plan education programs around them to appeal to the family.

2. What is the family-life coordinator?

Since Vatican II many parishes have added a new coordinator to their parish workers—the family-life coordinator. This person is responsible for planning programs that will appeal to all members of the family. In some parishes there is a family-life team appointed for this role rather than one individual.

3. How can I work with the parish family-life program coordinator for the good of the parish?

All of us can use our talents to provide programs for the families in our parish. As a DRE I would direct the educational programs, while the family-life coordinator would be responsible for the social aspect. For instance, we could have a pot-luck supper. After the supper there would be a guest lecturer for the adults and an educational experience for the children. I'd contact the speaker and make all the arrangements for that portion of the evening. This would include planning something for the children, such as a movie or a supervised activity. And the family-life coordinator would take care of all the details of the pot-luck supper, such as table arrangements, sign-up sheets, etc.

4. What if the parish doesn't have a parish-life coordinator?

Unfortunately all parishes do not have a parish-life coordinator or team. And yet this is an area we need to concern ourselves with if we are to minister to families in our parish. As a DRE it's to your benefit to have someone to coordinate family programs with your education programs. You can either approach the pastor or pastoral council with a request for such a position or take it upon yourself to find a person for this role—someone who can work with you. There are training programs at the diocesan level for people wanting to work in this area. There is even a family-life office to turn to for help and guidance.

5. Are certain times of the year better for scheduling family-centered programs?

Yes, looking at the seasonal calendar gives us a good starting point for our family programs. There are the seasons of Lent and Advent which precede the major feasts of Easter and Christmas where we can plan a family day of activities in preparation for the feasts. Remember the days when such activities were discouraged during Lent? And we can't forget to make the best use of summer times as good family-programming time. Spreading family-centered programs throughout the year will add a special dimension to your church activity calendar.

6. How can we include single adults in our family programs?

It's very important that singles do not feel left out of our parish programs. With the emphasis on family, this can happen if we don't make a conscientious effort to include them. This means single parents as well. No longer can we say "family" and mean the unit with mother, father, and children. Family must have the broader meaning to include all who live together in a household. If your parish is small enough, you'll have the advantage of knowing those who live alone or are single parents. And you can personally make sure they are invited to be part of family programs. In larger places this is more difficult, but that just means we have to make a concerted effort to publicize that *all* are welcome at the family evening. In either case, inclusion for all should be our byword.

7. Why are potlucks a natural for family programs?

Most people like to eat, and it's fun to share our meals with others. Since everyone brings one dish, as you do in a potluck, you are sharing both food and fellowship. If you've been involved with parish potlucks you'll know they are great occasions for getting to know new parishioners as well as good community builders. And when you want to add some enrichment, you already have your audience for a lecture or movie series. Schedule your lecture or movie after the meal at a specific hour, allowing for clean-up time. Those who prefer to come for the educational portion can join the group at that time.

8. I feel that our parish is potlucked out. Can the potluck supper be abused?

Yes, as good as potlucks are for family and community building, they can become an ugly word. I've only seen this happen when they were *overused.* And in cases like this, the solution was to discontinue them for a while or get imaginative such as having a theme, or ethnic dinner. Start up when the people begin asking for them again. In the interim you could plan other parish gatherings, such as picnics or wine and cheese parties.

9. Our annual parish festival is coming up. How should I get involved?

It's really up to you how much you get involved in the parish festival. I've seen DREs taking a booth in the festival where the proceeds were for the benefit of the religious education program, and others working as members of the festival team where the proceeds were for the development fund and all ministries would benefit. Some DREs don't get into the working end of the festival, but otherwise give their support. It's important to be there, in whatever capacity you have chosen, because you are part of the parish family. And people look to you in your leadership role, whether it be directing a program or participating in an event.

10. Why should I schedule family retreats?

Family retreats are meant to bring several families together to pray, to work, and to play. They are significant in forming *community* among parishioners who may only see each other at weekly liturgies. If you are in a position to set up retreats for families, by all means do so. However, this is a big undertaking, and you'll want to get others to work with you, for there are too many dimensions to tackle this one alone. Again, if there is a family-life team they're a natural to join hands with you in this venture. They can plan the logistics of food and accommodations, while you take charge of the presentations and activities for all ages. There are many books available on setting up retreats which you'll want to refer to in preparing for this spiritual renewal.

11. My parish has a good-sized teen population. How can I involve them in these family programs?

There are two ways that teens can be part of our family programs. The first is offering talks, movies, or discussion groups for them while the adults are meeting. The second is tapping their talents for working with the younger children who are attending the event. There should be a balance of both usages so that the teens can grow from being nourished and from ministering to others. During family retreats they work well with younger children on field trips and in activities. During lecture series provide them with an opportunity to share with other teens. We need to remember that teens don't fit naturally into adult discussions or feel comfortable being placed in the children's section. They need their peer group for support. But they should also be part of the total group. This applies at liturgies, celebrations, and, of course, at meals.

12. Why is scheduling so important to family programming?

Our lives seem to revolve around the family kitchen calendar. If you want to get families to your programs, you'd better put your bid in early for a date on that calendar. You're competing with scouts, sports, dancing or piano lessons, and school functions, just to name a few events. In fact, it's a good idea when you begin planning for family programs to consult the local school calendar so you won't be doubling up on PTA night or open house or the homecoming football game. Many times we think people don't want to come to the parish potluck or religious education family session, when in reality it was poor timing on our part.

13. Are there any adult education series especially geared for parents?

There are a number of series designed for adults to help them in their role as parents. The most popular are the series by James Dobson and Clayton Barbeau. These are now in video form, but can also be obtained in 16mm film for parishes where this is preferable. They are set up in a series to allow for ongoing study and discussion. Most dioceses and Christian church centers have them through a rental system. However, there are rental agencies to obtain them from if your local area does not have them. Although these are the most popular, the market is unlimited. Refer to catalogues and diocesan publications for the latest programs available to your parish.

14. Do all programs for the family have to be scheduled at the parish center?

No. There are family programs that lend themselves to the home. I am referring to home masses, small neighborhood discussion groups, and Bible study gatherings. The informal atmosphere of the home can make these occasions even more meaningful. I've found that many times a good discussion group in a home is much more meaningful because people feel more at ease in sharing and there are no time restrictions as occurs when using parish facilities. And if the group is from the same neighborhood, it's helpful for babysitting and building neighborhood friendships.

15. What can I offer mothers who have young children at home and are unable to attend the parish classes?

For years I've conducted mothers' coffee groups for just this reason. When I was at home with my little ones I was searching for a group to share more than the latest cure for diaper rash. Since there wasn't such a group already in existence, I took it upon myself to start one in the local parish. We gathered at my home in the beginning, but eventually everyone took a turn hosting the morning session. The children were able to come and were given

---

EXTENDING COFFEE GROUP ACTIVITIES

Sometimes when a group meets for a couple of years, there is a bonding that extends beyond just coffee and discussion. Recently this happened in our parish. The group happened to be mothers of young children. They had met for two years, and as they approached the summer of the second year, they wanted to continue to meet through the summer weeks. During the year their children were taken care of in the nursery while they had their faith sharing sessions. During the summer they would schedule their gatherings around the children's interests. Each Wednesday morning they met at the parish hall and proceeded to the day's activity. In order to make it possible for all to participate, they alternated free activities with those which cost a fee. Their excursions took them to such places as the zoo, the museum, the shoe factory, and the bakery. It was a special time for the children and their mothers. And it strengthened the bond of this community as they moved back into their faith sharing when school started in the fall.

a place to play while the adults carried on their discussion. Naturally there were a few distractions, but it was worth it. I've continued to form coffee groups everywhere I go—we've moved seven times in the past fifteen years—and I still believe they are one of the best modes of adult education for young mothers.

16. How should we use the liturgical seasons of the year for family programs?

Both Advent and Lent are good times to invite families to come together for sharing ideas on how to make the most of each season. Either on or before the first Sunday in Advent, plan an Advent-Wreath-Making Day. Families can gather at the parish hall with their own materials, having been given instructions in the parish bulletin. Simple activities for the younger children can be organized while the adults and older children make the wreaths. It's also a good opportunity for the pastor to mingle with his parishioners and to bless all the wreaths at the end of the activity. And depending on what time of day, refreshments or a meal could be included. This is only one of several options for an Advent Day. As for Lent, the same type of approach could be used, with families gathering before Ash Wednesday for creating home projects such as Lenten calendars, a Lenten cross, or another related activity. There are many books with creative ideas for special liturgical events throughout the year.

17. Is there a problem in setting up family programs when one of the spouses is of another faith?

There shouldn't be—but we must be sensitive to this issue because it can create problems. Now, more than ever, we have large numbers of parishioners who have spouses from different religions. When we set up family programs it can be a good opportunity to welcome that other member into our parish gathering. This is especially true if that person is attending his or her own church on Sunday and we never have contact. It also helps the children in these families to see that our church wants to bring families together.

18. Can we offer programs to meet the needs of families where one spouse is of another faith?

This is one request I have heard more than once from couples. We set up classes called "Inquiry" for adults wanting to find out more about our religion with the thought of joining. But what about the folks who aren't of our religion and just want to learn more about it—with no plans on joining? It's a real need which begs for our attention. Another area we should look at is how to help parents bring their children up in one religion when the parents practice different religions.

19. Can we tie in any family activities with the Sunday liturgies?

One popular practice for families on Sunday morning is gathering for breakfast or brunch. The parish can capitalize on this by offering breakfast right at its own facility. Pancake breakfasts and breakfast tacos can be set up as community events as well as fund-raisers for different parish organizations. The religious education program should support these family times. I've found that setting up the year-round schedule to allow for one Sunday a month to be designated as "Family Sunday" without regular classes is popular among both teachers and children. This is the Sunday you would schedule the parish breakfast.

20. What do you mean when you say "Family Sunday"?

In 1978 I walked into a program of Family Sundays in Omaha, Nebraska and I've taken it with me in every program I've started since then. If you conduct classes between September and May (which most programs do) there's a natural break in almost every month for a free Sunday. That's the Sunday we call "Family Sunday." We cancel the regular classes and encourage families to spend some *quality* time together. The catechists and helpers like this idea because they can plan their out-of-town trips for this weekend or other activities for the family. And, of course, the children like this concept because it makes a break in their usual Sunday classtime—a free day from RE. You'll find that it also helps attendance on the regular Sunday classes. I strongly encourage DREs to consider this practical step in their scheduling.

12
Sacramental Preparation
Let's Get Parents into the Act

One area of church life the DRE has a great impact on is in the planning, organizing, and conducting of classes for parents in sacramental preparation. With the directives of Vatican II reminding parents that they are the primary educators of their children, DREs are responding by helping parents fulfill this challenging role. In reality, much of our religious education program revolves around preparing children, teens, and adults to receive one of the sacraments. How to be effective in this area is the subject of this chapter.

1. What sacramental preparation programs should I be responsible for?

Almost all DREs are responsible for preparation programs of children receiving their first eucharist, for those preparing to receive the sacrament of reconciliation, and for teens preparing for the sacrament of confirmation. Some are also asked to help in programs for parents who bring their children for baptism as well as adults seeking entry into the church. To avoid confusion about who is responsible for sacramental preparation, it's a good idea to specify in your job description what sacramental programs will be your responsibility.

2. Why are the sacraments the focus of much of our religious education program?

We are a sacramental church. Our emphasis and involvement in the life of the church are related to the sacraments. Some of this is due to the education and emphasis we experienced in our own sacramental life growing up in the church. Thus we see parents coming to us with their children to prepare them for the sacraments. In fact, ask any DRE what classes are the largest in our programs. Invariably they will be those preparing for first eucharist or reconciliation. And in high school it will be the confirmation group. Because we see this situation, we should make our sacramental preparation programs worthwhile. Then parents will want to continue in the religious education program beyond the reception of the sacraments. This is a prime time to educate parents on the importance of an ongoing education.

3. Are there any diocesan or deanery guidelines to help with sacramental preparation programs?

Most dioceses and deaneries will have guidelines for parishes to use in setting up programs. However, these are only guidelines, not regulations. One reason for these guidelines is to discourage families from "shopping" to find a parish where they can have a quick celebration for baptism or the eucharist without a proper preparation period. There will always be individual circumstances that will necessitate exceptions in preparation for a sacrament. You can deal with these as they occur. Your requirements for preparation classes should not be merely "checking a box" but rather helping both children and adults. This will be accomplished if we provide worthwhile classes as well as good experiences of prayer.

4. Can the deacons assist in sacramental preparation programs?

Yes, they are a great asset in the sacramental preparation programs, and to ignore them would be a shame. This is one area where deacons can work on both sides—in preparation as well as in celebration—of the sacraments. For as deacons they will also be involved as celebrants. I've always worked closely with deacons in the classes of preparation for infant baptism. And I've seen what a help they've been to pastors as they've taken on pre-marriage preparation. Whenever possible, work with your deacons and invite them to use their particular gifts to prepare both children and adults for the sacraments.

5. What are some of the needs I should be aware of as I plan a baptism program for our parish?

If you are called upon to work in the baptism program, there are needs that are unique to this group. You'll find many young couples returning to the church, after a period of separation, asking to have their child baptized. You must be sensitive to this and *warmly welcome* them back to the community. If you set the right environment, they will feel more at home. Your leader couples and others in the group can help these young couples share their faith life. Because you are working with parents of infants, be sure to make allowance for parents who wish to bring their babies with them, and try to provide babysitting for the other toddlers in the family. When you set up your schedule, you'll want to keep your meeting time to a reasonable length—one hour, no longer than an hour and a half.

6. Should I invite couples to help in our parish baptism program?

Young couples ministering to other young couples—that's what it's all about in sacramental preparation. Although you'll be asking the pastor or deacons to assist, don't leave the entire task to the professionals. It's not fair to the parents coming to the classes, or the parents who would like to lead these classes. Ask several couples who have young children to act as leaders—then take time to train them. They can lead the first session on Christian parenting. This is especially welcomed by first-time parents. During this initial meeting, they'll also want to address any sponsors who are

SCHEDULE FOR BAPTISM PROGRAM

Evening #1

Welcome parents and godparents.

Presentation by leaders: Christian Parenting.

Opportunity for sharing.

Instructions on filling out information sheets needed for baptism certificate.

(Optional) Presentation and explanation of bib or stole for baptism.

Concluding remarks and passing out take-home sheets.

Evening #2

Welcome couples/sign in.

Presentation by the priest or deacon on theology of baptism.

Opportunity for question and answer period.

Concluding remarks and passing out take-home sheets.

Evening #3

Welcome and sign in/sharing.

Presentation on the rite of baptism today.

Tour of church.

Walk through the baptism ritual.

Question/answer period, dismissal.

(If you prefer to meet only twice, combine the session on the theology of baptism with the explanation of the rite.)

present concerning their role as godparents. If you schedule your leader couples in teams, they can alternate in leading the sessions.

7. Will I be running programs for adults seeking admission into our faith community?

You may be. It depends on how your pastoral team is set up. In smaller parishes DREs tend to take on more areas of responsibility since the staff is smaller. If you are asked to work in the RCIA—the Rite of Christian Initiation of Adults—you'll find it invaluable to attend an institute for preparation. We no longer merely "instruct" adults in doctrine for a few months and bring them to the font of baptism. There's a rather lengthy period of preparation and candidates are asked to walk this journey of faith through the different stages before becoming part of a new faith community.

8. When should I begin classes for children to prepare them for receiving their first communion?

Every September you'll receive calls from concerned parents saying, "My child is ready for first communion. What do I need to do to get her into your class?" It's almost like clockwork—second grade going hand in hand with first communion. Most parishes schedule their preparation for first eucharist in the second grade. But we are seeing a change in policy emphasizing longer preparation periods—with a two year rather than one year preparation for the eucharist. They are requiring that children be enrolled in classes for one full year before they move into the eucharist class. Thus if children come to you in second grade with no previous religious education, they will move into the eucharist class in third grade. No matter what age and grade you schedule your preparation for the sacrament, you'll want to include parent classes in your program.

SACRAMENTAL PREPARATION EVALUATION

1. What did you like the most about this program?

2. If you could change any part of the preparation, what would you change? Explain.

3. Rate the following: *Very good   Good   Fair   Poor*
   a. Children's materials:
   b. Parent handouts:
   c. Opening prayer services:
   d. Parent sessions:
   e. Children's class sessions:
   f. Joint sessions parent/child:

You may add any other comments on the reverse side.
                     Thank you for your cooperation!

Name: (optional)

---

9. How can I set up classes to involve the parents in the sacramental preparation?

Parents are the primary educators of their children. This is especially true in preparation for the sacraments. You can help them in this role by providing classes for them. During these classes you'll want to give them directives for working at home with their children. At the same time, you'll be able to present an update on eucharistic theology. I've had many positive experiences with parents during these sessions. Many come to these classes to fulfill a requirement, but they leave them extremely grateful for the experience. In some parishes I have asked only the parents to attend the meetings, giving them materials for home use with points to help them, while in other parishes both children and parents come for the evening session. After an initial welcome and prayer, the children go to classrooms for their lesson while the parents stay in the hall for their presentation. Either approach has values. You need to decide which fits your particular needs.

10. What should I do about the children whose parents do not or cannot attend the required classes?

This is always a difficult question and does not have a black and white answer. Certainly you don't want to deprive these children from receiving the sacraments because their parents are uncooperative. Each situation must be looked at individually and handled with extreme sensitivity. There are parents who *cannot* attend evening classes because of other demands, such as jobs, family needs, etc. I've worked with these parents on an individual basis. We arrange to meet at a time convenient for both of us. But there are those parents who *will not* attend meetings because of other reasons. Some are angry at the church, yet they don't want to deprive their children of the sacraments. We need to take time to invite these parents to return to the community. Many times a child's first eucharist will bring parents back to the church. When others refuse to attend, we can only pray that they will support their children. We can invite the godparents to assume this role in the parents' absence.

11. I find that parents are concerned when to prepare their children for the sacrament of reconciliation. Are there some directives to which I can refer?

The big question on reconciliation is where it belongs. I've worked in some parishes where it preceded first eucharist—in the second grade—and others where it was after first eucharist—in the fourth grade. This is confusing to families who transfer into new parishes. They wonder: What *does* the church teach? As DREs we must follow the directives of the diocese or parish we are working in. In the catechetical sense, there are reasons pro and con for both times of preparation. Seven year olds are certainly not going to be guilty of serious sin, but they do have a sense of sin. Therefore, there should be catechesis on sin and forgiveness at their level. This can be followed by a communal service of reconciliation rather than individual confession if this is preferred. If individual confession is desired, it should be kept very simple for the young child. Some pastors prefer to wait until a later age, such as ten or eleven, before children have individual confessions. At this age the child is more aware of sin and more able to benefit from the reception of the sacrament. When we meet with parents we should emphasize the positive reasons for receiving the sacrament at whatever age your diocese directs.

12. Is it possible to involve the entire parish in our sacramental preparation programs?

Yes, it's not only possible, but it's strongly encouraged to involve the parish in the sacramental preparation programs. This can be done through including enrollment ceremonies for the candidates preparing for the sacraments in the Sunday liturgies. In many parishes, prayer partners are taken from the community for candidates preparing for the eucharist and confirmation. The candidates are also mentioned in the prayers of the faithful during the months of preparation.

PRAYER PARTNERS

Below are two suggestions for having prayer partners for candidates preparing to receive one of the sacraments.

1. *Involving Every Parishioner:*
   a. Take each candidate's name and make multiple copies of it. You can do this by taking a sheet of paper and repeating the name about fifty times, then cutting the sheet into pieces with a name on each piece. If your parish is extremely large you can duplicate the sheet the number of times necessary to have a name for each parishioner.
   b. Pass a basket with all the names of the candidates and have each parishioner take one of the names. This will be the person you will pray for.

2. *Involving a Limited Number of Parishioners:*
   a. Have a poster or a banner with the candidates' names on it displayed somewhere in or near the church.
   b. Invite parishioners who would like to be a prayer partner for one of the candidates to select one of the names. This will be the person you elect to be a prayer partner for.

13. Are there any secrets for surviving the overwhelming tasks at sacramental preparation time?

It usually happens every spring. There are groups preparing for first eucharist, teens preparing for confirmation, and adults preparing for entry into the church. As a DRE you're involved with all of it! The secret to survival is *delegating.* You must recognize your limitations. Each of these preparations is a full-time job. Taking care of

SACRAMENTAL TEAMS' JOB LIST

Mark the person(s) responsible for each of the duties below:

Before the Sacramental Classes:

1. Compile list of families with children who will participate in this program: _____

2. Help with mail-out to these families: _____

During the Classes:

3. Check baptismal certificates: _____
   (Eucharist and Confirmation)

4. Collect fees for materials: _____

5. Record attendance at sessions: _____

Before the Celebration:

6. Help with overall liturgy preparation: _____

7. Work with children doing readings: _____

8. Organize the offertory procession: _____

9. Set up the seating plan for the church: _____

10. Instruct and work with ushers: _____

11. Prepare flowers or other special decor: _____

During the Celebration:

12. Help children with processions: _____

13. Set up for the reception: _____

14. Serve refreshments: _____

15. Clean up after reception: _____

all of them is just too much for one person. You need to bring in others to help in the extra tasks before, during, and after the sacramental celebrations.

14. What are the specific tasks I can delegate?

I like to have sacramental coordinators as well as special teams to help with each sacrament. I work closely with these teams. They can take care of the paperwork, such as checking baptismal certificates, marking attendance records, and collecting fees. Meanwhile, you can put your energy into presenting theology classes for the parents. During the celebration of the sacrament, you need to be available for coordinating while your team members take care of setting up for the reception, working with the candidates who have a special role in the celebration, and taking care to clean up afterward.

15. When should I begin preparation for the sacrament of confirmation?

Confirmation is now being celebrated in most parishes during the high school years. This is quite different from years past when it was received during the elementary school years. Most programs of preparation extend over a two-year period and include prayer, studies, and service involvement. If you are responsible for setting up the program for confirmation, check deanery or diocesan guidelines. Then schedule your program to comply with them and your own parish needs.

16. How can I involve the parents in this program?

It is important to bring parents into your confirmation program. Unlike working with parents of children receiving the eucharist, you'll be dealing with parents of teens who aren't as comfortable having their parents involved in their faith life. You can do this in a non-threatening way by inviting the parents to an orientation to explain the total preparation program. Some catechists have groups of teens and parents working together during the classes, while others prefer to combine groups only at special rites

---

FAMILY BANNER MAKING

An added touch to sacramental celebrations or other family events is having a homemade banner. In our first Eucharist program, we give families a banner kit with some helpful hints during the preparation period.

Kit contents: One piece of beige burlap 12″ by 24″

Letter patterns
(optional—you can make your own)

Instruction form

Instructions for banner making:
1. Decide on the words and symbol for your banner.
2. Fray the edges of all four sides of the banner by pulling individual threads so you have a frayed edge of ½ inch.
3. Cut out the letters and symbols from your own materials.
4. Glue or sew these on.
5. Mark your child's name on the reverse side with a marker or pen.

Bring your completed banners to the final parents' meeting. They will be hung on your family pew for the celebration. You will be able to take them home as a keepsake on that day.

throughout the preparation. They can be included as prayer partners during the months preceding the reception of the sacrament. Further, they can work with their sons and daughters making stoles, banners, and other items needed. Just because teens and parents may need a little support at this age is no reason to leave them out of this important phase of their faith journey.

17. Can I combine the religious education and parochial school sacramental programs?

Yes. In fact, if we move into a parish where they are still celebrated separately, it's time to change. Hopefully your influence will cause this to happen. There have always been problems in parishes where there is both a parochial school and a religious education program. However, we are seeing a movement where these programs are beginning to work together. It would seem only natural that both programs celebrate the sacraments as one. Ask teachers in each program to work with you. When you set up parents' meetings, you'll want to invite all the parents to participate. This lays the groundwork for having the classes come together at the end for the celebration.

18. Since the pastor is ultimately responsible for the celebration of the sacraments he should be included in the preparation. How can I involve him in this process?

It's important to sit down and talk to the pastor about the parish policies on the sacraments when you begin working in a new parish. This is one area where you'll be working together. Many times setting up the schedule, providing classes for the children as well as the parents, and taking care of all the details of the celebration will be your responsibility as a DRE. But you'll want to include the pastor in the classes for parents and children, giving him an opportunity to get to know the families. In many parishes, where the numbers are not overwhelming, the pastor will meet the children through individual interviews before the reception of the sacrament. In preparing the liturgy, you must include the pastor to avoid any embarrassing moments where he doesn't know what's happening. If everyone has prepared together, your celebration will be a positive experience for all!

19. What can I offer adults wishing to return to the church?

We need to respond to the growing numbers who are returning to the church. Most of these people have been away from the church for some period and are now ready to approach the church. We must do more than just open the door and slide them into the pew. There are usually hurts to be healed, experiences to be shared, and relationships to be reconciled. After an initial interview, we can invite these adults to come together with others who are returning to the church. This newly formed group should be led by adult members of the community who are ready to listen to their stories, give them some theology on the church today, and answer their questions. And when they are ready, they will rejoin the community at the table of the eucharist.

20. Are there any sacramental preparations I shouldn't get involved in?

You may feel you're involved in all the sacrament programs. However, most DREs are not responsible for marriage preparation or the sacrament of the sick. This is where deacons are most helpful and effective. In many parishes you won't be responsible for preparation for baptism of infants or adults. You'll be able to decide with what sacraments you can be of help once you've been working in a parish for a few years. Don't overextend your ministries to the detriment of the traditional religious education programs.

13
Summer Activities
What About *My* Time Off?

Summer is a welcome time of year for the DRE. It's probably the only time you can slow down a little. The programs for the year have ended. Yet there are programs that are perfect for the summer schedule of families in your parish. To pass up this opportunity is a mistake I have found that DREs make. Sometimes we're too anxious to close shop. Or maybe we just feel everyone is "programmed out" for the year. Let's take a fresh look at how to make the best of summertime for parish activities.

1. What programs lend themselves to summertime scheduling?

Some of the best programs of the year can be summertime activities. In these programs, with a more relaxing pace, learning takes place in a casual environment. They can be children's programs, family activities, or adult gatherings. With the school year over and the children at home all day, parents always *welcome* these programs.

2. When should I begin planning for summer programs?

Your long-range planning should begin in early spring—March or April. At that time decide what type of program to offer, as well as what materials to order. It's also time to start looking for summer coordinators. If you're having separate programs for the children, for families, and for adults, you'll want to choose a different coordinator for each area. After you've decided upon your schedule, your materials, and your coordinators, you don't need to meet again until a month before the programs begin. At that time, work closely with your coordinators to select activity center leaders for the children's program, to recruit teachers and helpers for all the programs, and to set up registration dates.

3. I'm strapped for volunteers. Should I dare ask my year-round catechists to work in the summer program?

Most certainly! Welcome them to participate in this program. They have the advantage of already knowing many of the children, and if their children will be participating, it's convenient for them to be there. However, try not to limit this experience to your regular catechists. There are often many parents and teens who will help during the summer who can't help during the year.

4. Why should I get the teens and pre-teens involved in the summer program?

They like it! And it's great to see them relating to the little children. For many it's their first opportunity to be on the "teaching side" in the religion program. In the beginning the younger teens will need to work under the supervision of adults. The pre-teens can work as aides in the different centers, while the high school teens are ready to actually teach or lead a group activity. Those who enjoy this experience will be first to volunteer for the following summer. And some of the teen teachers will want to teach in the year-round program because of their positive experiences in the summer program.

5. Should I charge a registration fee for the summer program?

Yes, because paying a fee is making a commitment. And this money will be needed for ordering materials, supplies, and snacks for the program. The registration fee should be reasonable. However, no one should be deprived of participating because of the cost. And the RE budget can underwrite part of the expenses if necessary.

6. Since the summer program is different than regular classes, how should I set up the schedule?

I have always liked using a rotation method for scheduling during the summer program. The children gather in a central area for music and prayer during the first half hour. They depart this area—beginning with the youngest age group—and move to their first interest area. They continue to rotate to the designated activity center each thirty minute period. The three and four year old groups need to be a little more flexible because these children are so young. The movement from classrooms for lessons, to arts and craft centers, to the outdoors for snacks, music and play, makes for an interesting morning—a pleasant change from sitting in a classroom for two hours!

7. What time of summer should I set up our children's program?

I've always found the best time is usually two weeks after their public school classes have been dismissed. After two weeks of vacation time the children become restless and parents are anxious to have them spend their energy outside the home. If you have an early summer program, you can get serious about cleaning and closing up for vacation once the program ends. I know some parishes prefer the latter part of summer. However, I've found that between July and mid-August most families go on vacation. And by August you need your energies to begin preparation for the new year.

8. How long should our summer program run?

Some schedule their program for two weeks, others for one week. I prefer something in between—eight days. I've found that one week is not long enough and two weeks is too long for both children and workers. Therefore, the eight day schedule—from Monday to Thursday for two weeks with a three day weekend in between—seems to work best for everyone. But if it's your first experience of a summer program, you might want to begin with only one week, lengthening it the following years.

9. What materials should I order for the summer program?

Every year new materials are being published for summer programs for children. You'll want to set up your goals for the program before you select the curriculum materials. Some programs emphasize scripture, while others are based more on daily Christian life experiences. Every few years you may want to change the approach to add variety to your program. Your budget may also dictate the type of materials to order. One helpful hint: each year have your teachers and helpers evaluate the materials at the end of the program. That will be your best guide for next year's order.

10. Why is this a perfect setting for creative activities?

You'll have the luxury of time and space for creativity. Now you can take on projects you wouldn't dare tackle during the year—like finger painting, casting molds, and sewing banners, etc. Both the arts and crafts and music sessions should be structured to enhance the faith-sharing times. The little ones delight in bringing home their "creations" to display on the family refrigerator. And the songs taught each day are echoed in the homes throughout these weeks.

11. Do liturgies fit into the children's programs?

Each morning you'll want to begin with a short prayer or prayer service. As a closing to your program, it's fitting to have a longer prayer service or celebration. This is also a fitting time to have a children's liturgy. It's a great opportunity for creativity. The children can take responsibility for both preparing and participating in this liturgy. They can incorporate the projects created throughout the week as well as the new songs that were learned. You'll want to invite the parents and other family members to this celebration.

12. Are there other ways to conclude your summer program?

Yes. I've seen everything from an evening program with the children performing, to an afternoon carnival where each grade sets up a booth for the families to gather for fun. Other types of celebration are a liturgy followed by a picnic, a program of each class presenting a song or skit on the final day, and a program written by older children but including the younger children. You can use this closing celebration to present awards and give gifts of appreciation to the workers. No matter what type of celebration is planned, you'll want to invite the parents and families.

13. What other programs can we set up for families during the summer?

One parish I worked in set up family programs with the family ministry team members during the summer. Once we had planned the program for the summer, the couples took over since the times coincided with my vacation plans. Just because you're

---

SUMMER EVENINGS

You can set up six evenings of movies and games for the families in your parish. Gather the families at the parish hall for the showing of a 16mm film or video. You can have a separate movie for the adults in one room and one for the children in another nearby room. Or you may want to show a family film for everyone to enjoy together. Make sure to have popcorn and iced tea and drinks for all. On the alternate weeks, you can set up the volleyball net for either outdoor or indoor games. While the adults play volleyball the younger children can be supervised on the playground area.

Another variation for summer parish evenings is having potluck suppers one evening each week during the month of July. You can invite interesting guest speakers to these evenings to share their expertise in talks after the meal. You'll want to have movies or other entertainment for the children during these talks. The idea for all these evenings is to provide something for the entire family.

---

not there doesn't mean programs must stop. These evenings of families gathering were welcome during the summer when there were no pressures of the school year.

14. Should I consider having adult education courses during the summer?

This may be one area you'll want to avoid scheduling formal classes at the church. Just look around at your Sunday liturgies in the midst of summer and you'll notice many families absent. Vacation times and family trips interspersed throughout the summer months make it impossible for most adults to make parish commitments. However, you can encourage adult education by setting up small discussion groups in different homes. When you schedule these, you may wish to use the subdivision and neighborhood layouts for planning purposes.

15. I'd like to attend some summer school classes. How does that fit into my schedule?

Most colleges and universities will offer classes that will help you professionally. Because your summer commitments are less demanding, many DREs take advantage of this opportunity for their own personal enrichment. It's probably the only time you can give the time and energy needed to do justice to your studies. However, don't overextend yourself by taking on too much. And be careful that your duties to the parish don't suffer because of your class schedule.

16. Is summer a good time to schedule in-service programs?

It's amazing how many adults have more time for in-service during the summer months. They're even ready to attend evening sessions. When a group of volunteer teachers were asked for a time they would like a series of workshops, the majority asked for Saturdays during the summer between 8:00 a.m. and 2:00 p.m.— and their attendance was outstanding! Another time I scheduled theology updates on Wednesdays during June and almost all the teachers participated. All this seems to say that summertime *is* a good time for in-service.

SCHEDULE FOR TEACHERS' RETREAT

Friday, August 11
6:00 p.m.   Meet at parish center—carpool to retreat center.
7:00   Gather at center, unpack and get settled.
7:30   Relaxation time: walking tour, video.
About 10:00   Evening prayer service before retiring.

Saturday, August 12
8:30 a.m.   Breakfast in dining room.
9:00   Morning prayer.
9:15   First Presentation "Our Faith Journey."
10:00   Activity: Charting your faith journey.
10:45   Coffee, tea break.
11:00   Sharing.
11:30   Reflection on scripture.
12:00 p.m.   Lunch in dining room.
1:00–3:00   Recreation time (walking, swimming, reading, etc.).
3:00   Gather in meeting hall—presentation on scripture.
3:45   Scripture activity in small groups.
4:30   Sharing.
5:00   Closing prayer service.
5:30   Supper preceded by social.
6:30   Departure from retreat center.

17. What about teacher retreats during the summer?

The flexibility of family schedules allows more adults to take a day off or even arrange for an overnight stay during the summer—something that isn't possible during the school year. Although a weekend retreat would be more beneficial, it's too much to ask families to give up Mom or Dad that long. I've had more luck scheduling the retreat over a twenty-four hour period—beginning Friday evening and ending Saturday evening. If you can arrange this retreat to take place in more informal surroundings—at a lakeside or rustic area—you'll have a perfect setting for renewal as well as relaxation. These retreats are valuable times for personal growth as well as great community builders.

18. How can I take care of ongoing programs of formation during the summer months?

Some programs aren't scheduled on a nine-month cycle. Programs such as RCIA (Rite of Christian Initiation of Adults), the classes for baptism preparation, and any other adult programs should be able to continue during the summer months. That doesn't mean that you as a DRE must be there to supervise them. If these programs fall within your job description, you should have coordinators to assist you in directing them. Summer is a good time to ask these coordinators to take responsibility for these classes. Some coordinators schedule less frequent meeting times for these groups during mid-summer because of family vacations and the availability of the participants. You don't want to keep a program from meeting because you're on vacation.

19. Why is August planning so important?

It's during this final month of summer—before classes begin—that we can make all those final plans and preparations for the upcoming year. Even though pre-registration has been completed, temporary class lists have been made, teachers have been recruited, and schedules are in rough draft, you aren't ready to open for your first classes. It's time to send out letters with schedules to all families registered in the fall program and tie up the loose ends.

20. What activities should I schedule during August?

This is the time to get your teachers and helpers back together. By mid-August most families are back from vacation and are getting serious about pre-school plans. Your teachers will be anxious to come together for some in-service. If you can schedule a series of two or three meetings, you can begin preparing your teachers for the upcoming year. And you can avoid the last-minute panic before classes begin in September. But August should not only be time to work together. We should also gather to have fun together. If you can have a "welcome back" cookout or potluck supper to bring the teachers and helpers together, you're setting the mood for a good year.

14
Liturgy
Let's Make Those
Special Liturgies Special

As a DRE, you will no doubt be asked to plan liturgies throughout the year. These will range from the opening of classes and special feasts on the church calendar to special celebrations for the first reception of the sacraments. Fortunately, you don't need a degree in liturgy for these tasks. However, you'll want to seek volunteers with gifts and talents in liturgy to create an atmosphere to make each liturgy special. Let's look at how this can be accomplished.

1. How can we create liturgies for special celebrations?

We do not create liturgies, such as the eucharistic liturgy. The liturgies have already been established by the church. What we can do, however, is select music, prayers, and atmosphere to make these celebrations more meaningful. Our intent should be to involve the children and teens in the planning and participation in the liturgy as much as possible.

2. I don't feel comfortable putting together a liturgy. Why can't I just follow the missalette?

The missalette does have the readings and parts of the liturgy in accordance with the day of the year. But that's about all it has. In many ways it's a deterrent to our participation in the liturgy. We find parishioners reading along with the lector instead of listening to the word being proclaimed. However, if you're uncomfortable planning your own liturgy, you can use the missalette as a beginning for the scripture readings. But don't stop there. Guide your students in creating their own prayers of the faithful and prayers of thanksgiving. Gradually you can add music, special processions, liturgical dance, and movements that fit the celebration. And you can guide your students to set the atmosphere through banners and posters.

3. Why is it important to work closely with the pastor or celebrant when working on liturgies?

The celebrant not only needs to know what is going on, but he should have some input into planning special celebrations. It's not fair to the celebrant to tell him at the last minute what you plan to do during his liturgy. And yet that's what frequently happens. When you're planning something special, it's a good idea to meet with the celebrant several days before the actual celebration.

4. Why should I involve the children in the liturgy?

I notice two things happen when children are involved in liturgies. First, they begin to understand its meaning. They see how each of the different parts form the whole. As they prepare to do the readings, they get experience using the scriptures. Second, they enjoy taking a more active role in it.

5. What steps can I take to involve the children in liturgies?

There are many ways children can learn about liturgy. They can begin by taking part in the entrance or offertory procession or by saying one of the petitions. Eventually they can write and read their own petitions. As soon as they are able to read, they can do the scripture readings or act out the meaning of the scriptures as they are read.

6. I find that there is a problem with children *performing* rather than participating in a prayerful manner during special liturgies. How can I resolve this?

This is a danger when children are responsible for parts of the liturgy and the adult community is also present. Young children standing at the lectern can give the impression of being "on stage." It's important to warn against this. This starts with our attitude in preparing the children for their role. We should help the children proclaim the word—presenting it prayerfully. If we pay too much attention to what the children wear and the externals, they will believe that they are performing. This is especially true at times of first celebrations of the sacraments. If these are to be family celebrations, we'll want to keep the candidates with their family, not separating them because it looks nicer that way.

7. Are there specific times during the year that lend themselves to special liturgies?

Yes, there are those times you'll want to make liturgy special. Some of these are the beginning of the school year, the holidays of Halloween, Thanksgiving, and Christmas, the seasons of Advent and Lent, the celebration of receiving a sacrament for the first time, the closing of the school year, and the summer vacation program.

8. Can I ask my catechists to plan their own liturgies?

By all means. You'll want them to help with liturgies because they already know the children. However, if you are fortunate in having a children's liturgy team, don't forget to use their resources. They can work with both the catechists and the children. I have found this to be an effective way of using the combined talents of the liturgy team and the catechists. Each is grateful for the support and assistance of the other.

9. How can the liturgical planning teams meet the needs of the different age groups in the parish?

One approach for meeting this need is to divide the liturgy team into groups according to the different age groups. Delegate a group to take care of the overall needs of the community. But add a youth team for the teens and a children's group for the younger members. All the teams can meet monthly to plan the parish liturgies with a look at the special feasts and the features of the liturgical calendar for that month. After that each group looks at how they can implement these into their particular group's liturgies.

10. Are there any resource materials I can refer to in planning children's liturgies?

Yes. Religious book stores and catalogues offer numerous books to help in both the planning and the conducting of children's liturgies. There are also religious education and liturgy periodicals to address this need. You'll want to take advantage of these resources in your planning. Many offer successful programs. Why not learn from those in the know?

11. Why are some parishes offering a special liturgy of the word for the young children during the Sunday liturgy?

This is designed to help children grow through understanding the scriptures. One of the major emphases in the liturgy since Vatican II has been its effort to revive interest in the scriptures. We are reminded that we are nourished by the eucharist *and* the word each Sunday. However, the word in scripture and its explanation in the homily is on an adult level. More and more parishes are responding to the needs of children by offering a separate liturgy of the word for them.

12. How can I introduce this practice in my parish?

Before you introduce this practice, you'll want to be well read on it. And you might want to go to a parish that has already implemented this practice. After you've done your homework, present your ideas to the pastor or pastoral team. With their support, you're ready to turn to others for help—the liturgy team, catechists, and adults interested in working with children and scripture. Before you actually begin, inform the parish at large of the program. This can be done in a short presentation at all the liturgies. Then, if you've been able to sell it, begin!

13. What materials are available for setting up a liturgy of the word for children?

There are books that have sample sessions to use for a liturgy of the word for children. They are usually divided into sections for pre-school, primary grades, and middle grades. Begin gathering

---

GUIDELINES FOR SETTING UP
LITURGY OF THE WORD

1. Set up a prayer table: with cover, Bible, candles and any other decor.
2. Use music for background.
   (May prefer to open with a song)
3. Read opening prayer to the children.
4. Lead children in penitential rite.
5. Teacher or child proclaims the first reading.
   (Use either the Old Testament or New Testament reading for the day)
6. Sing or recite responsorial psalm together.
7. Leader proclaims the gospel.
   (Gospel can be dramatized, or presented through media)
8. Recite a simple profession of faith.
9. Children recite their petitions.
10. End liturgy of the word with a song.

---

books and periodicals on this subject for resources. You can keep them in a small box which can be transported between your home and the place of children's liturgy.

14. How can I involve the teens in the parish liturgy?

You'll want to work with the parish liturgist in bringing the teens into an active role in your parish liturgy. Some parishes designate one of their weekend liturgies for youth participation. They are responsible for the music, the readings, welcoming and ushering, and acting as eucharistic ministers at this liturgy. Other parishes prefer to integrate the teens in all their liturgies, giving them the responsibility for these same ministries alongside the adults. No matter what approach is taken, it's important to show the teens that they are important in this ministry and not just substitutes because of a shortage of adults.

15. Many times retreats with teens conclude with a liturgy. How can we help make this a positive experience?

This is a great opportunity to truly celebrate a liturgy with teens. After spending many hours together in prayer and play, they gather together with a bonding as a community. They are ready to celebrate! It's their celebration of life, centered in the eucharist. As they sing, and pray, and share, they are prepared to break bread together. If the celebrant for the liturgy is present for part of the retreat, you'll want to have the teens work together with him in the preparation and planning stage. If he is not present, an adult can take over the role in order to ensure that the liturgy is relevant to the weekend experience.

16. Why is selecting the right music important in planning liturgies?

Music is important because it sets the tone and atmosphere of the celebration. Children's music and teens' music are not usually the same. And there are different types of music that appeal to groups within the adult community. Fortunately the quality of church music is improving. When deciding on the music for a particular liturgy, be mindful of the theme of the scripture readings as well as the age group participating. Most parishes take this into account as different liturgies become characterized by their music—folk music, children's choir, organ background, etc.

17. I've seen bulletin covers used during special liturgies. Why are these good media to use?

They are professional in appearance, a practical size, and are printed to follow the liturgical year including special feasts and sacramental celebrations. Their convenient size works well for printing the parts of the liturgy. If they are being used for a celebration, this is one way of listing the names of children participating in the celebration.

18. What celebrations lend themselves to using bulletin stock?

There are covers for seasonal holidays, such as Thanksgiving, Christmas, and Easter. And these are the times when your liturgy usually has additions or notations which you'll want to print on the handouts. I've also found that they are helpful for celebrations of first eucharist, reconciliation and confirmation. Families and friends appreciate these handouts. It helps them follow the liturgy and it's a nice keepsake of the special event.

USING BULLETIN COVERS FOR PROGRAMS

The format for your special liturgy can be printed on the inside of bulletin stock. If you need three half pages, make sure you order bulletins with the illustration on only the right side. Some covers are printed across the entire front side leaving only two half pages for your program.

SAMPLE:

First Eucharist Celebration
December 13, 1989

WELCOME

ENTRANCE PROCESSION:
Celebrant with children in the communion class.

OPENING SONG:
Great and Wonderful

1ST READING:
1 Corinthians 11:23–37

RESPONSORIAL SONG:
For You Are My God

2ND READING: Romans 12:9–18

GOSPEL: Luke 7:18–22

HOMILY

PRAYERS OF THE FAITHFUL

PRESENTATION OF THE GIFTS—
assigned students carry the gifts as we sing: *Love One Another*

Holy, Holy, Holy—sung

COMMUNION SONG: As the children approach the table of the Lord with their families, we shall sing: *One Bread, One Body*

CLOSING PRAYER

RECESSIONAL SONG:
God's Blessing Sends Us Forth

☐ ☐ ☐

MEMBERS OF THE EUCHARIST

(Print Children's Names)

☐ ☐ ☐

EVERYONE IS INVITED TO JOIN US FOR A RECEPTION AFTER THIS SPECIAL LITURGY

19. When should I use para-liturgical rites in the religious education program?

There are times when the community gathers for prayer but not necessarily for a eucharistic liturgy. Some of these gatherings call for a special rite or service. There are special rites to prepare candidates for the sacraments. They are modeled on rites in the Rite of Christian Initiation of Adults (RCIA) such as the rite of acceptance, the rites of reconciliation, and the rite of enrollment of candidates. But there are numerous other occasions when we can gather and pray with the children, teens, and adults throughout the year. We should be attentive to making ritual part of our religious education program.

20. How can I work with the parish liturgy coordinator?

If your parish has hired a liturgical coordinator, you should count your blessings. Your program will be enriched by using this resource person. So much of religious education can be tied into the liturgical life of the church. You can work together to plan parish celebrations around the seasons and feasts of the church year. And you'll be working not only with the coordinator but hopefully with the entire liturgy team.

15
Publicity
When You've Got It, Flaunt It!

In our religious education programs we spend many hours planning, preparing, and organizing in order to succeed. However, we don't seem to put the same energies into publicizing what we have to offer. Our efforts to spread the word are minimal in comparison with our efforts to create programs. A few lines in the parish bulletin, a Sunday morning pulpit announcement, or a quickly created flyer is usually a last minute attempt to inform our parishioners of our newest program. If we truly believe in our product, why are we so hesitant to promote it? How to increase our communication skills and achieve better results is the focus of this chapter.

1. How much time should I spend on advertising a new religious education program?

This is hard to say. Much depends on the nature of the program. But if we believe we have a good product, we need to let others know. This means planning ahead. Advertise a new program at least one month before it begins. And use a variety of media to do this. You might even want to use some witty "coming attraction" techniques to spark an interest.

2. Can you give me some suggestions on how to pace this advertising?

It's a good idea to use "one liners" several weeks before your program opens. As you come closer to the dates for the program you'll want to increase your scope with a variety of techniques. Large and attractive posters stationed near the church entrances will catch the attention of those attending the liturgies. Some parishes have invested in large signs and billboards that can be seen by all who pass by. Having handouts professionally printed with more details on the program makes a statement of its importance. If you are going to have a sign-up day, don't forget to have leaders and knowledgeable folks around to answer questions and assist in the process. It's wise to attach a fee to enrollment. As I've said before, in our society, money means commitment.

3. How can I reach the non-church-going parishioners?

A parish mailout is one way to insure that all registered parishioners get information on programs and classes. However, this is not usually done for every program because of the expense involved. Some parishes publish a newspaper either monthly or quarterly. This is an excellent tool for advertising programs. Many times there are non-church-going parishioners living near those families who regularly attend. We need to challenge these families to reach out to their neighbors, inviting them to become active in the community. There's nothing as effective as a personal invitation.

4. It seems that most people don't read the Sunday bulletin. Why should I bother to publicize any religious education programs in it?

There are some people who read it and use it as their main source of "what's happening" in the parish. We can't expect to reach everyone through one medium. By using the Sunday bulletin as a means of publicity, we have a central place to refer to. Many times I've advised callers seeking future information to "watch the Sunday bulletin" for more details. And you have a response for the upset parishioner who complains "No one told me what time the class started!" by stating what bulletin it was printed in.

5. Should I use the church bulletin board for publicizing religious education classes?

By all means! I think you can learn about a parish by studying the bulletin board at the church entrance. You'll want religious education classes and programs right up front with the news from the different parish organizations. But if you do post programs and classes, keep your listings up to date. Notices about programs and events left on the board weeks after they have ended give our parishioners another message—one we don't want to give!

6. Our parish sends out a quarterly newspaper to all registered parishioners. What type of religious education material can I include in this?

This is a great way to show the entire parish what's happening in religious education. Pictures of celebrations, programs, and activities, with an explanation accompanying them, are a vehicle for sharing the event with the group participating as well as the remainder of the parish. It's a good idea to invite participants in these programs to also submit their writings. I remember that during the first years in the RCIA the candidates were willing to share their faith journey with the larger community. The newspaper is also an effective way to promote upcoming programs and events.

7. Is it difficult to print a newsletter exclusively for religious education?

No. In an age of computers and copy machines we have the equipment to do the job. The question is whether we have the volunteers willing to tackle this project, and whether we are able to support them with leadership and direction. You probably don't want to add this to your job description, but you can delegate this task if someone is interested and talented in this area. This is an area where the children and catechists can contribute. Their classroom experiences and their creative works can be printed for all the families to enjoy.

8. What about a newsletter for youth?

A great idea! And the teens like it too! You'll have teens in your program who are familiar with journalism in their school. Tap their talents! If you have a youth coordinator, encourage the teens and coordinator to share their programs, their views, and themselves. They can circulate it either to all the youth in the parish or to the larger church community—whichever they prefer.

9. How can I have my programs included in the weekend pulpit announcements?

Each parish has its own policies in this area. You'll want to check on how you should write up your announcements, noting if there are restrictions. It's important to follow the directives on when these announcements should be submitted in order to be read on a certain date. Here you'll need to plan ahead.

10. Why are some pastors opposed to Sunday morning pulpit announcements?

I've heard pastors complain that pulpit announcements are ineffective and distract from the spirit of the liturgy. If they are presented by the commentator before the liturgy begins, many don't hear them because of movement about and late arrivals. The alternative is to take a few minutes before the closing prayer and hymn.

However, there are also distractive movements and early depart-
ers to contend with. Again, each parish has to decide how to best
use announcement time, realizing its limitations.

11. Am I responsible for all the publicity for the religious ed-ucation program?

Yes, ultimately you are the one who is responsible for the publicity of your programs. But that doesn't mean you personally have
to do it! You can either delegate this task to someone who likes to
do public relations or have a committee spend its energies on
publicity. When a group is involved in the process, they can divide the work among themselves—one group for the bulletin
board, another for posters, etc.

12. Should public relations or advertising be built into my annual budget?

Yes. You'll need supplies in order to operate. There will be poster
board, markers, chart holders, and other materials for your dis-
plays. If your budget can handle it, it's a good idea to have bro-
chures and flyers printed throughout the year for special programs.
The cost of mailouts—stamps, paper, and printing—should also
be considered when calculating your budget.

13. What's the best way to distribute flyers to parishioners?

There are many ways to distribute flyers to your parishioners. The
way you distribute the flyers will depend on the audience you are
trying to reach. If the information is for the families in the religious
education program, you can send the flyer home with either the
youngest or the oldest child in class. Or you can mail to these

same families. To include the larger parish family, you can mail it to all registered parishioners. However, to keep the expense down, you might want to include it as an insert in the Sunday bulletin. Another system is placing flyers on car windshields during the Sunday liturgies, if that's within parish policies.

14. Should I use more than one means to advertise programs?

Yes, don't be satisfied with only one approach. You'll want to use a variety of means in order to reach the maximum amount of people. However, don't use the same media for every program. You can overdo printing flyers and using bulletin inserts. And some programs deserve more attention than others. If you're starting a completely new program, you'll want to spend more energy on publicity. Programs that recur only require reminders in the bulletin or through your newsletters.

15. How can I involve the children in getting word out about programs?

Young children seem to be the best messengers for spreading the news. And because they are, I like to send flyers home with the youngest child in the family. For years I gave this responsibility to the eldest child attending classes. However, I learned that not all the messages arrived home.

16. What other groups can I turn to for help with publicity?

Your key group, of course, will be those who have volunteered to be part of your publicity committee. But in order to be effective they should make contact with other organizations. So many times in church ministry one organization has little idea of what the other is about. By approaching the organization leaders, you

---

ADVERTISING THROUGH PARISH ORGANIZATIONS*

One way to communicate to parishioners about upcoming programs or speakers is through the established parish organizations. Here are some of the ways you can approach an organization:

1. Contact the chairman of the organization, explain the program you wish to advertise, and ask to speak at their next meeting.
2. Send a representative from your R.E. board to meet with each of the different organizations in the parish to promote your upcoming program.
3. Meet with the different organizations' leaders, present your program, and ask them to explain it to their organizations and pass out handouts.
4. Write to each of the organizations requesting some PR for your program. You might want to enclose flyers as well.

* You would not want to do this for every program, but only for special programs once or twice a year.

---

can advertise your programs to all the members of that group. And hopefully these members will continue to spread the word throughout the entire community.

17. When should we advertise beyond the parish community?

If we are bringing in a noted speaker or a workshop team to help our volunteers, it would be a nice gesture to invite our neighboring parishes to participate. Depending on the nature of the program, this could include many parishes. The same is true if we are hosting a speaker for the teens. Why not share our resources? We don't do enough of this! By publicizing beyond our parish, we are increasing our audiences, and usually decreasing our expenses.

18. Is there a way I can evaluate how effective my advertising is?

By its results! Are people getting the word? Or is the expression "I never know what's happening" the norm in your parish? In your evaluations at the conclusion of your program or classes include a question pertaining to how they heard of the program. This will give you an idea of what advertising works. When only a small number appear for a new program, there's a good chance that the publicity was inadequate.

19. Are these evaluations really necessary? Most people don't want to take the time to fill them out.

If you never ask the question, you'll never know the answer for poor communication. You can be wasting valuable time and energy on advertising that gives poor results. If flyers are left in the pews or on the parish grounds, you may want to try another source for publicity. Using the input from your evaluations will show you where to concentrate your future efforts.

20. What do you feel is the best way to advertise in the parish community?

I've found that the most effective means of spreading the word in the parish community is through personal contact. People sell the program to other people. If your program is good, the word will spread. However, no amount of advertising will bring results if the product isn't worth having. In most cases we do have a good product. However, we don't always put the effort into telling our people. We need to challenge our captive audiences. Then every time we repeat a program, we will increase participation.